# Alex Smith

*a biography*

# Alex Smith

*a biography*

## BY HEATHER SIMONSEN

spring creek
BOOK COMPANY

Provo, Utah

© 2005 Heather Simonsen

All Rights Reserved. No part of this publication may be reproduced in any form without the written permission of the publisher.

ISBN 13: 978-1-932898-34-7
ISBN 10: 1-932898-34-4
e. 1

Published by:
Spring Creek Book Company
P.O. Box 50355
Provo, Utah 84605-0355
www.springcreekbooks.com

Cover design © Spring Creek Book Company
Cover design by Nicole Cunningham

Cover photo © Getty Images
Back cover photo and interior photos courtesy of Pam Smith.

Printed in the United States of America
10 9 8 7 6 5 4 3 2 1
Printed on acid-free paper

Library of Congress Cataloging-in-Publication Data

Simonsen, Heather, 1970-
Alex Smith / Heather Simonsen.
   p. cm.
ISBN-13: 978-1-932898-34-7 (pbk. : alk. paper)
ISBN-10: 1-932898-34-4 (pbk. : alk. paper)
1. Smith, Alex, 1984- 2. Football players--United States--Biography. I. Title.
GV939.S624S56 2005
796.332'092--dc22

                    2005006808

# Table of Contents

# A Note From Alex Smith

This book came to fruition through the dedication, hard work and creativity of my cousin, Heather Simonsen. Heather has known me all of my life and she has seen me grow into the person I am today. She approached me after the 2004 football season wanting to chronicle my progress and the inevitable ups and downs of my journey to Salt Lake and to the University of Utah. I appreciate Heather and her desire to put my experience onto paper for others to share.

My journey and the success that followed could not have been possible without the unbelievable support of the people of Salt Lake City and Utah fans nationwide. My decision to attend University of Utah was one of the best decisions I have ever made. The memories I created there I will carry with me forever. I was able to grow as a student/athlete, but more importantly, as a person. However, this entire journey and where I am today has been a team effort. That team starts with my family and in particular, my mother and father. My parents instilled in me the importance of hard work, discipline and education. They are the foundation with which I have built my life and will continue to do so.

My family also consists of my older brother Josh, my older sister Abbey, and my younger sister, MacKenzie. Josh has always been my hero even though he had the propensity to put me in a red wagon when we were kids and send me down the hill unaccompanied. Abbey has always been my protector, looking out for me and always there to catch me at the bottom of every hill.

Last but certainly not least, my little sister MacKenzie is my partner in crime. She gave me the gift of being an older brother and

ALEX SMITH

gave me the opportunity to push the wagon instead of being in it.

I hope this book gives the reader some insight into my humble experience as a student/athlete. I did not expect to have a book written about me at such an early age with so much yet to accomplish. I consider this to be only the beginning and I am excited about what the future has in store.

With that said, my cousin Heather has done a wonderful job chronicling an amazing chapter in my life and hopefully there will be many more chapters to come.

Sincerely,

Alex Smith


*All of Alex's proceeds from this book will be donated to a charity.*

# Acknowledgments

Our grandpa died before Alex was born. I remember clearly the sunny summer day in Idaho Falls when Grandpa asked my twin sister, Holly, and I to take an ice-cold soda to the boy who was mowing his Technicolor green lawn.

I replied inquisitively, "Why don't you take it to him, Grandpa?" He answered with a smile, "Because it will taste better coming from you." It was the first time I began to understand a woman's power. I hope this book honors grandpa's memory.

Alex's mom exemplifies the power of a woman. Known as "Sweet Aunt Pam," she nurtured the inner strength and character that led to Alex's phenomenal success. When Pam is in the room the colors are brighter. She's the super glue that keeps our family intact. Always the one to organize a dinner out or activity, Pam is a friend to everyone—little children and the elderly alike. Thank you for your devoted assistance in the book's research process. I love you, Pam. This book is for you.

Uncle Doug is Pam's handsome, athletic husband. I remember when I was eight years old and my mom had cut my long, blond hair. Doug told me convincingly that it made me look "more mature." I felt grown up for weeks. Doug builds confidence in others. It's hard to measure the ripple affect Doug has had on students as the principal at Helix Charter High School. Doug takes school administration personally and the world is a better place because of it. Thank you, Doug, for the in-depth interviews you've given for the book.

Pam and Doug have four children who are not only successful individuals, but are also a tight-knit family group who enjoy spending time together. I send love and gratitude to my cousins Josh, Abbey and MacKenzie for all your keen insights and candid responses.

I'm grateful to my uncles Gene Barnes, Ronnie Barnes, and Steve Barnes for sharing with me their tender memories of Alex as a child. Thanks also to Alex's uncle John L. Smith for taking time out of his busy coaching schedule at Michigan State to share some colorful stories.

I wish to thank Alex's high school coaches: Jim Arnaiz, Robert Berg, Ron Boehmke, and Gordon Wood for providing me with insights into Alex's first years playing football. Gratitude to his teachers and administrators: Mimi Test, Gifford Asimos, Ben Stone, Jane Huntington and to Alex's best friend David Edwards. Many thanks to Alex's University of Utah football coaches—Bill Busch, Urban Meyer, Dan Mullen and Kyle Whittingham—who took time from their frenetic recruiting schedules to talk to me for the book. I appreciate Chris Hill, the University of Utah's athletics director, for his glib and warm remarks. I thank Alex's teammates Tommy Hackenbruck, Matt Kovacevich, and Morgan Scalley for their compelling comments.

Thanks to my husband Soren for his support in writing this book and for being the sunlight of my days and the solace of my nights. To my adorable "peeps," Halle and Christian, for pulling up their little table and drawing next to me while I wrote this book. They sat wide-eyed at the dinner table each night asking to hear another "Alex story." Halle and Christian, I love you up to heaven and back.

Most of all, thank you, Alex, for giving me the opportunity to write your story. You will inspire many people to conquer their own challenges and reach high into the heavens to obtain their goals.

I recall the night during winter semester of his sophomore year when Alex came to our house to retrieve the big-screen TV his parents had given him for Christmas. We had been storing it for him during the holiday break. It was so large and heavy that it took both my husband and me to slide it across our hardwood floors.

When Alex arrived, it was snowing heavily outside. I tried to help him carry it down our granite steps to the car, but my side wouldn't even budge. Alex arched over the TV, lifted it up and carried it down the slippery, snow-covered steps as easily as one would carry a stack of books. I remember being amazed by his strength, thinking to myself, "I bet he's going to play really well next year."

And then he pulled away in the dark during a snowstorm without his headlights.

Heather Simonsen
March 2005

# Chapter 1

# THE CELEBRATION AFTER
# THE FIESTA BOWL

No one thought they could do it.

The magnetic allure of the 2004 University of Utah football team—led by their shy, cerebral quarterback, Alex Smith—captured the nation's imagination as the team charged toward an undefeated season. The quintessential underdogs completed the regular season with an 11-0 record and became the first mid-major team ever to be invited to play in the Bowl Championship Series. Critics questioned the Utes' qualifications to play in a BCS bowl. Were they really good enough?

When the BCS bowl bids were announced on national TV, the Utes learned they would be playing on New Year's Day in the Fiesta Bowl in Tempe, Arizona. Under the leadership of head coach Urban Meyer, they would face the Pittsburgh Panthers, champions of the powerful Big East Conference. This was undoubtedly the biggest game in the history of the University of Utah football program.

Tickets for the game quickly sold out, and when the game began, the stadium looked like a sea of red because of the record number of Utah fans who donned school colors and traveled to Arizona to watch their team. In fact, so many people drove the eleven-hour journey from Salt Lake City to Tempe that a popular restaurant in Page, Arizona, ran out of pies for the first time ever.

At least three-fourths of the 73,519 people in the stands were cheering for the Utes.

The fans' loyalty was amply rewarded. A national TV audience watched in surprised awe as the Utes jumped to an early lead under Alex's calm leadership. The Utes' defense masterfully kept the Pittsburgh offense in check, and the Utes steadily put points on the scoreboard. As the game rolled on, the TV commentators focused more and more on Alex, offering their opinions that he had the right combination of skill, confidence and leadership to succeed as an NFL quarterback.

As the game concluded, the Utes had fashioned a convincing 35-7 win, leaving the nation impressed and leading to a No. 4 ranking in the final Associated Press poll, the highest ranking by a mid-major team in many years.

Even before the Fiesta Bowl, the awards started spilling in. Alex, once the gangly third-string freshman quarterback who wasn't heavily recruited by other colleges, won several major awards, including national Player of the Year honors from both *Sports Illustrated* and *The Sporting News*. He was also named as an Academic All-American Player of the Year, and finished forth in the balloting for the Heisman Trophy. Local sports writers deemed him the best football player *ever* to play at the University of Utah.

It was a surprising journey for this overlooked recruit, who had been teased in high school by fellow students and players. Many people had claimed he was only the quarterback because his dad was the principal. These critics weren't aware of Alex's scrupulous devotion to the game. He meticulously studied game film, and he regularly consulted with his coaches to understand the offense and to anticipate the opponents' defensive moves. He put in the sweat equity when no one was watching, and it had paid off. The clumsy little boy from San Diego who used to trip over his own feet had become a champion.

"When I was a little kid, I couldn't have drawn a better picture of what the dream would've been like," Alex said. "I'm so thankful for my life. There are a lot of things that had to go right to get me here. I've been so fortunate to have the family I have and to live the life that I've lived."

Kyle Whittingham, the University of Utah's defensive coordinator in 2004 and now the school's head coach, summed it up this way: "People will be talking about this season for many years to come. This was a magical season."

## A SUBLIME TRIBUTE

As the Fiesta Bowl began to wind down, the thousands of Utah fans in the stadium remained in their seats. Alex's coaches wanted to give him a special moment on the field where the fans could cheer Alex's accomplishments and let him leave the field a final time. Dan Mullen, Utah's quarterbacks coach at the time, remembered the decision to give Alex that special tribute.

"Coach [Meyer] said, 'Let's leave him in the rest of the game,'" Mullen recalled. "I said, 'Coach, I'm gonna put [Alex] in for a couple of plays and take him out so he can give his final farewell to everyone, to let him come off the field victorious with a single moment of attention.' I wanted Alex to have that moment. I knew it was the end of my time at Utah. I had a good feeling that it was the end of his time."

Alex remained focused on the game, unaware of what was about to happen. "Coach Mullen told me that I was going back in to play," Alex remembered. "To then be pulled off as they announce your name, and then to run off and see coach Meyer, I felt complete joy."

As Alex walked off the field of his final college football game, the stadium announcer boomed "Alex Smith!" into the microphone and the crowd erupted into a standing ovation.

Mullen, known as a player's coach, remembers feeling a kind of happiness similar to a proud father watching his son succeed. "To see him be able to walk off that field victorious was unbelievable," Mullen said with emotion. "I'm probably as proud of him as his parents, just to see how far he'd come in two years. To get him to finish his career as the best, undefeated, it was great."

When he left the field, Alex first embraced Meyer and then gave Mullen a big hug.

"By that point, I knew that was probably my last college game," Alex recalled. "To end it at the Fiesta Bowl was such a climax of everything."

## A ROUGH START

The relationship between Coach Meyer and Alex had actually been rocky in the beginning. Alex wasn't Meyer's idea of an ideal quarterback. Meyer considered him to be too slender, and he didn't have the high school stats to prove his talent.

"He was an okay quarterback who overanalyzed everything and didn't know what he was doing that first spring," Meyer said. "But he was a great kid."

Alex remembers feeling discouraged by Meyer's disapproval when Meyer took over as head coach. He was also leery of Meyer's trademark intensity. Fans had given Meyer the nickname "Urban Legend" because of his highly disciplined coaching style that consistently turned a losing team of talented athletes into winners.

Alex later came to appreciate Meyer's emphasis on hard work and discipline. Through that embrace at the Fiesta Bowl, the unlikely friends demonstrated the ultimate respect they had developed for each other.

"We had come so far together," Alex said. "I'd become close to him over the last two years. I think he understood as well that I was moving on. There was a lot of emotion."

Meyer remembers the intensity of that moment. "I was ecstatic that we did our job. I was very proud of our players."

A sports photographer snapped a photo of Alex and Meyer embracing. The next day, that photo made the front page of sports sections across the nation.

Alex's older brother Josh Smith couldn't keep his emotions inside as he watched that moment. "I was bawling," Josh said. "I think I'm a tough guy, but with stuff like that, forget it. It was unbelievable," he said. "I was so proud of him. I was telling all my friends, 'Take your real pictures and mental pictures—it doesn't get any better than this.' I was soaking it all in through my tears."

Alex has extremely close-knit relationships with all three of his siblings, but Josh is his biggest fan. Though eight years apart in age, they used to create plays together when they played impromptu backyard football games.

Brains and athletic talent run in the family. Josh earned a bachelor's of science degree in neurobiology and physiology, and a master's degree in public health. He's currently pursuing a PhD in epidemiology. Josh played football in high school and at the University of California at Davis before sustaining a severe ankle injury that permanently sidelined him. Josh says he was ready to give up football and has never looked back, but his experiences helped inspire Alex to set high goals.

Alex simply hoped to one day be good enough to play college football. In his wildest dreams, he never imagined he'd achieve so much in the sport, but football is in Alex's blood. His father, Dr. Doug Smith, EdD, coached high school football in Idaho and Washington and also coached for two years as a graduate assistant at Colorado State University.

Another key influence was Alex's uncle, John L. Smith, who is the head football coach at Michigan State University.

"College football was the dream," Alex said. "So many things happened, but nothing is greater than the actual games. That's why I put in all the work."

Alex's mom, Pam Smith, remembers how her son fought to reach his goals throughout the 2004 season. Only two years before, he had considered transferring to another university. A coaching decision to put him in a game at San Diego State—in front of Alex's family and friends—cost him his redshirt year. He struggled in his college football debut and it stifled his confidence.

Pam always believed in her son's abilities and knew he was gifted, but in remembering the challenges of that first season, even she was surprised at how far he'd come. When she watched Alex receive the Fiesta Bowl tribute from his coaches, Pam was thrilled beyond words.

"It's hard to describe how much joy you get from it," said Pam, a 25-year veteran of the Social Security Administration, and currently Deputy Director of Health and Human Services for San Diego County. She has also served in an elected position on the school board for more than ten years.

"It was his dream," Pam said. "The bad first year was in my mind. Maybe the bad makes you appreciate the good. To be part of something great at the University of Utah was spectacular."

Pam added, "Life is full of different stages. A lot of stages blur as your kids grow. This was a moment where you could say: 'next stage.' I wanted the team to win and I wanted Alex to have a good game because it might be his last. He showed all of his talents. He had a spectacular game. I was so happy for him."

## RUNNING TO THE STUDENT SECTION

Alex is shy and reserved, a man of few words. All season long he kept his emotions in check. But after he left the field, he could no longer keep it all inside.

"Coach Mullen and I talked about how the student section had been so good to us and that we needed to go celebrate with them," Alex said. "I struggled with it. I like to stay low-key during the game and stay even-keeled."

After the last play of the game, Alex showed a rare firecracker of emotion. "There was nothing stopping me at that point. I was so fired up," he remembered. "I went nuts."

Alex's older sister Abbey Smith watched from the stands in shock. The scene is etched in her mind.

"I don't know if many people saw it. Alex doesn't show much emotion even when they score a touchdown," said Abbey, who is five years older than Alex and the Director of Sports at the South Bay Family YMCA. "He ran over to the student section and threw his helmet. It was neat to see his emotion and to end the game on such a high note."

When they were kids, Abbey took on the mother-hen role with Alex. She always tried to keep him safe while rambunctious Josh took Alex on adventures.

Josh remembered his brother's outward expression of jubilee with the students. "It was completely out of the ordinary," Josh said. "It really made me understand that he understood the moment. Sometimes he remains so calm when I'm thinking, 'How do you do that? This is such a huge moment.' For once you could see he understood the moment. It was also a little bit of a good-bye. It meant that he'd probably be leaving."

Though he hadn't yet announced his decision to leave Utah to enter the NFL draft, Alex knew he was leaving college football forever. Alex had earned his undergraduate degree in two years with high honors, an accomplishment that led his teammates to call him "Doogie Howser" after a popular TV character who was so bright he had attended medical school as a teenager.

Alex had already far surpassed the goals he'd set for himself, but it wasn't a simple decision to leave Utah while he still had a year of eligibility remaining. He knew college football provided an experience and atmosphere like no other.

Pam said, "It was a great way to wrap up one phase. It was a well-thought-out decision to leave. It was a clear decision, but it wasn't easy. It wasn't going to be easy to tell people he'd grown to love."

Alex said he ran over to the student section to demonstrate how much he had appreciated their loyal support.

"They've been so great this whole year," Alex said. "I won't find that in the pros—that energy the college atmosphere has. There's so much pride and you play for so much more at the college level. In the NFL, money gets involved and there's not that sense of unity that there is on campus."

## SWEET REWARDS

Once the Fiesta Bowl had concluded, Alex walked onto the stage with his teammates. He had been named offensive co-MVP of the game with his teammate and favorite receiver, Paris Warren. Another teammate, Steve Fifita, had been named the game's defensive MVP.

Alex's emotions were close to the surface as he held his MVP award and the Fiesta Bowl trophy. From the twelfth row of the stadium, his younger sister MacKenzie Smith cheered him on.

"When Alex took the mike to be interviewed as one of the game's MVPs, the whole stadium started chanting 'One more year,'" remembered MacKenzie, who plays soccer for the University of California at Davis. Alex used to tote MacKenzie around to his sporting events when they were little and included her with his friends when he was a teenager—a time when many older brothers would just as soon leave their little sister behind.

"He wasn't handed this opportunity or the talent," she said. "He's worked for it. There's no other person I'd rather see this happen to. Not just because he's my brother, but also because he's a good person. It just goes to show that good things really do happen to good people."

It was all a whirlwind for Alex. "From me running off the field that last play and then running over to the student section, and then all the sudden I'm up on stage in front of a sea of red and they're presenting me the trophy," he remembered with excitement. "It was truly an honor to be up there with my teammates as ABC was presenting us with the trophy. It was pretty late by then, but none of the fans had left yet."

MacKenzie thought of the older brother with the big grin who protected her when she was a little girl. She had also seen him struggle. "It made it that much more sweet," she said. "We saw him two years before at the San Diego State game. This was so much sweeter. There was no better payoff for him than that, for all the fans to be chanting. It was pretty amazing."

Kyle Whittingham, who Alex deeply admires, said that the excitement that night was palpable. Whittingham had been in the trenches with Alex and his teammates, helping them achieve the Utes' first unbeaten season since 1930.

"It was incredible. It was the most satisfying moment of my career," he said. "To have it end with the Fiesta Bowl, with the atmosphere and electricity in that stadium, was something else. I was so excited for the players. It's all about the players. It couldn't have happened to a better group of players."

## A FATHER'S PERSPECTIVE

Alex's father Doug became so nervous before games that it often felt like he was getting ready to play himself. The accolades at the end of the Fiesta Bowl meant he could finally exhale.

"I was relieved that he had accomplished a great deal and much of what he wanted to accomplish with the team—a perfect season," Doug said. "You feel, as a quarterback's parent, that he has great opportunity to shine. But he also has great opportunity to have it not go so well."

Doug is known for his unique ability to connect with his students at Helix Charter High School, where he has been the principal for nearly two decades. Most days, Doug eats in the cafeteria with his students rather than in the teachers' lounge. He's often seen walking the school halls, demonstrating that to truly help kids you have to know them. Doug also spends his break time with the students.

He has a similar approach to parenting. On the surface, it might seem paradoxical: strict but loving, highly involved but able to let go enough to allow his kids pursue their dreams. But it's a winning combination.

"You do become nervous about how he's going to do and how the team is going to do especially at the end of an undefeated season," Doug explained. "That anxiety grew throughout the season. The pressure on the next game grows. I was breathing a sigh of relief that they had accomplished their perfect season and Alex had done well. I was extremely happy for him, happy that he'd gotten such joy out of the year."

Still, Doug's test for success is simple.

"People say, 'You must be so proud of your son.' I'm proud of what he's accomplished. I'm not so sure that a good performance in an athletic competition would make someone proud. I separate the two. I'm happy about accomplishments, yes, but what makes me proud of him has more to do with the kind of person he is."

# Chapter 2

# A TOUGH LITTLE KID

Pam and Doug didn't play Mozart or Beethoven for Alex at a young age. They didn't drill him with flash cards as a toddler. They were not the type of overzealous parents who would scream on the sidelines at Little League games. Pam and Doug were loving and supportive of their children, and they made it clear to them what was acceptable behavior in the Smith home—which wasn't always an easy task.

Alex was born in Bremerton, Washington, on May 7, 1984. Pam accepted a job with the Social Security Administration in Reno, Nevada, two years later. The family spent an enjoyable summer together in Reno, where they took frequent weekend trips to Lake Tahoe. But that September, Doug had to return to Bremerton to finish working through the end of the school year.

It was a tough year for the family being apart, but by May of 1987, Doug was finished with his responsibilities at school and was looking forward to reuniting with the family in Reno. But the SSA offered Pam a position in San Diego, California, so they all moved there instead. San Diego soon became their permanent home.

## TAMING THE TANTRUMS

The "terrible twos" are aptly named for most kids. This phrase was especially fitting for Alex. His parents could see the temper explosions coming on. Try as they might, they simply couldn't always ignore them. The determination and intense focus that

11

*Alex at 15 months in August 1985. He is standing
in the corner, refusing to obey his mother.*

later in life allowed Alex to achieve on the football field and in the
classroom made it difficult for his parents to control him when
he was two years old. Once he got his mind set on something,
Alex was resolute. Nothing could sway him from the focus of his
attention. Alex had what his dad called "kicking, lay-on-the-floor,
out-of-control tantrums."

"He was determined to have his way," Doug said. "It ran
squarely into my determination that he wouldn't."

The flare-ups were so bad by the time Alex was almost three
that Pam and Doug thought twice about taking him anywhere
outside the home. They didn't want to have to deal with his little
diatribes while trying to navigate the grocery store.

One day, the family had relatives over. The visit was going well
when something triggered one of Alex's tantrums.

"We tried everything and put him in the bedroom," Doug
explained. "He was crying and kicking. He was in the bedroom
and out of control."

Doug had an idea. Calmly, he walked into the bathroom and
turned the shower on COLD. Then he picked up his kicking,

screaming young son, carried him into the bathroom, and held him under the frigid cascade.

"I thought a good dose of cold water might bring him out of it. And it did," Doug said. "I just turned that cold water on and stuck him in there. I got a little wet too, up to my shoulders."

Doug's last-ditch effort ushered in a new era for Alex.

"It brought him right into a better state of mind. You could talk to him then. It was a total turning point," he said. "He never threw a lay-on-the-floor, kick-your-feet tantrum again."

The story of the cold shower is now a part of treasured family lore. Alex has heard it many times, though he doesn't recall the incident at all. "It's funny, and it must've done something," he said. "I can remember standing in the corner a lot when I was little. When my memory picks up, I was out of that stage. So I don't remember those stories, but it's funny to hear about it."

His parents knew they needed to channel his fierce determination. They had to teach Alex how to work through those intense outbursts without discouraging his natural ability to maintain focus and achieve what he wants.

"Being stubborn can mean you don't give in and don't get along with anyone," Pam explained. "It can also mean you're persistent and that you follow through and stay with things. Kids are who they are. He has that strong will. I have a picture of him standing in the corner in the living room because he wouldn't give in."

Pam and Doug taught each of their children from a young age to be independent.

"They had to take responsibility for themselves and have accountability," Pam said. "You give your kids leeway, but the boundaries are there. If they throw a tantrum and give in to them, they learn they can get what they want that way. It's tough love. As a parent, you've got to funnel their strengths into their successes."

## HIDE-AND-GO-SEEK

As a little tyke, Alex had a keen sense of direction beyond his years. This became apparent when a game of fun turned into a harrowing experience. Family members chuckle about it in hindsight, though no one was laughing at the time.

One-and-a-half year old Alex was playing outside the family's apartment building in Reno with his older brother and sister. Pam was pregnant with MacKenzie at the time. Nine-year-old Josh and six-year-old Abbey decided to play hide-and-go-seek with their baby brother. The problem was that when the game was over they couldn't find Alex.

"Josh thought I had him. I thought Josh had him," Abbey remembered. "An hour later we were asking, 'Where is he?' We totally lost Alex. We lost him playing hide-and-go-seek."

Abbey and Josh searched frantically for him.

In the meantime, Alex, a pudgy toddler who was also tall for his age, amazingly found his way back to their apartment on his own. The little blond boy walked through the front door and found his bewildered mother, who asked, "Where are Abbey and Josh?"

The two older siblings finally gave up looking for Alex outside. Wearing worrisome looks, Abbey and Josh went home to tell their mother what had happened. Luckily, when they returned, they realized Alex had already found his way home safely.

"We got in trouble," Abbey winced. "We got our butts blistered for it."

While Alex's memory of this incident eludes him, he certainly recalls his adventurous older brother and protective older sister.

"They toted me around everywhere," Alex said. "Josh was trying to do things to me and Abbey was trying to protect me. Josh wanted to put me in a wagon and push me down the hill. Abbey was trying to make sure I didn't get hurt."

Pam says that was the way it always was with her kids. Protective Abbey would carry Alex around like a little mother and Josh would coax him into trying daredevil tricks. Alex wanted to do what the older children were doing.

"He would tag along with these kids who were five and eight years older than him," Pam said. "He loved playing with them and with the other kids in the neighborhood."

## FAMILY TIES THAT BIND

The Smith family is a close-knit bunch maintaining strong relationships they nurtured over time.

When Alex was two, his baby sister MacKenzie was born. Alex blossomed into an easy-going middle child. A likeable child who drooled a lot when he slept, Alex loved spending time with his siblings. "You look over and he's got a pool of drool down his chest," Josh laughed. There's still a stain on the leather couches in the family's home in San Diego where Alex fell asleep and drooled all over them the very first night his parents bought the plush furniture.

Though he was laid-back and lovable, Pam and Doug didn't realize how gifted their son would become. They predicted that his height would be in his favor. "That was my only tip-off in terms of potential," Doug recalled. "We did the calculations when he was two and it projected him to be above 6 foot 2 inches."

Alex is now six foot four inches tall.

*The Smith children had this photo taken for their parents' anniversary. Alex, bottom left, was just graduating from high school.*

*At age 4, Alex takes a break from practicing softball.*

*MacKenzie, 2, and Alex, 4, flash those trademark Smith grins.*

*By age 5, Alex was already showing good passing form!*

His natural ability to stay focus remained.

Pam said, "If he was watching TV or playing a game, I'd say 'Alex, dinner's ready,' and he'd tune everything out, including me."

Alex's uncle Ronnie Barnes, an alfalfa and wheat farmer in Idaho Falls, watched Josh and Alex play football together in the backyard when they were little. "I noticed Josh would throw him the ball and Alex could zero in on it and catch it."

Josh was Alex's hero from the beginning. Alex admired him and wanted to be able to play football just like him.

Josh said, "We made up names for plays and everything. We would play against other neighborhood boys. We'd play football at every opportunity we'd get."

Ronnie noticed Alex's uncanny ability to concentrate. "He liked to be right in the middle of it." That observation of Alex's playing style has proven prophetic.

While Pam and Doug encouraged their children to try new things, they never pressured them to succeed. "Our kids were supported but never pushed. Alex took guitar lessons, but it wasn't his thing. You try to expose them to things and find what's going to be their niche."

They impressed two main principles upon their four children: be grateful for what you have, and always give back. They taught them these valuable lessons through example.

Alex's parents have been involved in their community since he was in elementary school. Alex attended school in the Chula Vista Elementary School District, where Pam remains on the school board today. He went to Sunnyside Elementary for kindergarten through third grade and attended Discovery Elementary for fourth through sixth grade. Along with her elected position on the school board, Pam served on the board of the YMCA and volunteered at the Salvation Army. She'd take her kids along with her to teach them by example.

"Alex was helping assemble toys for the Salvation Army at Christmas when he was little," Pam said. "We had a strong emphasis on community involvement."

Being active in life and learning by doing was important in the Smith home.

"Our family was never a sit-on-the-sideline kind of family. The kids learned to ski and golf at an early age," Pam explained. "We've always given them things to do instead of things to have for gifts. It's the doing that's important."

Gifts like tickets to sporting events and museums trumped toy trains and cars under the Christmas tree.

The family went skiing each Christmas together and took summer trips to Lake Powell for water skiing and to the Grand Canyon. They enjoyed frequent vacations in Idaho visiting extended family. Their favorite times together were spent playing volleyball in the back yard and barbecuing ribs.

"All four of them are really close," Pam said proudly. "They've been that way from the beginning. They genuinely love each other."

The children learned to form opinions independently and to be knowledgeable about current events. Politics was fodder for dinner table conversation. The kids sparked impromptu debates with their uncle Gene Barnes, Pam's older brother.

Pam has 25 years of experience with the SSA, working her way into management. As deputy director of San Diego County she oversees many vital community programs including public health, aging, and child protective services. When Pam returned home to

*Pam and the children pause during a family skiing trip to Squaw Valley, California. Alex is second from the right.*

*A family photo taken during a visit to the family condo in Big Sky, Montana. Alex is at the bottom right.*

her children each night, she didn't waste one minute of time with them.

"We always took our kids everywhere," she said. "If we were going to a basketball game, or a play, we took them. It was a lot of exposure to good things."

Schooling was always at the forefront of family life. The kids were expected to take responsibility for doing their own homework and studying for tests. They fostered close-knit family ties, while maintaining clear lines about rules and accountability. Putting education first came naturally to Alex.

"He's always really liked school," Pam remembered. "I've never had a teacher who didn't really like Alex. He was always very engaged in the classroom. Even in junior high, Alex loved it. A lot of kids struggle at that age. He's always been able to enjoy the moment and get the most out of it."

Along with their *carpe diem* attitude about life, Pam and Doug knew that their relationship with each other was the foundation for a happy family life.

"The best thing you can do for your kids is to love your spouse,"

Pam said. "You have to work on that relationship."

They also nurtured close relationships with extended family members and friends. Pam followed the adage of former first lady and current New York Senator Hillary Clinton: *It takes a village to raise a child.* She said family and friends had a big part in all of her children's upbringings, especially Alex. "Neighbors across the street would have cookies for him. He'd visit his grandpa in Idaho in the summers," Pam said.

Alex's uncle Gene, a retired district manager of the Seattle Social Security offices, lives in San Diego with his wife Dorothy. He used to pick Alex up from junior high school.

"I always had a well-buttered roll just out of the oven for him," Gene said. "He always liked that." Alex had a special relationship with Gene, an intellectual. They found a common interest in discussing world history. Through talking about past world events, Gene noticed Alex's sharp ability to reason.

"His favorite game was 'What if?,'" Gene explained. "We'd be talking about a significant event in history and we'd say how would history have changed *if?* What if a certain battle had gone the other way? How critical was that?"

## THE FIRST FOOTBALL GAME

Alex became a star in the classroom—a teacher's dream. He was like a sponge soaking up all the information each day. When his parents would ask what he had learned at school that day, instead of the typical uninterested shrug and "I dunno," he'd go into great detail telling them all about the stories he learned in history class.

His father said he thoroughly enjoyed school and always excelled. "He wasn't perfect by any means, but he always did well," Doug said. "There was never a course in school he didn't like. He liked all of his teachers. He seemed to be able to find good in whatever he was studying and whoever was teaching. It wasn't so much that he was smarter than the other kids, but that he enjoyed school so much. Because he enjoyed it, he did well at it."

But Alex was not a stellar athlete by any stretch. His uncle Steve Barnes, a retired fleet service manager in Boise, Idaho, went to Alex's very first football game in the eighth grade. "I thought he didn't have a chance of being a great athlete," Steve said. "He was kind of clumsy." A growth spurt left Alex tall and thin, with oversized, awkward feet.

Alex's uncle John L. Smith said, "He was a big-footed, big-handed and clumsy little turd. We'd tease him that if he ever grew into those feet and hands he could be something. His nickname was 'axe-handle' because he was just a string bean."

He played quarterback in the last game of his Pop Warner football season in the eighth grade because something happened to the team's quarterback. Alex hadn't played all season long. What's more, he'd never even practiced playing quarterback. The team hadn't done well that year. They lost that last game, too. Even still, Doug was surprised by how well Alex had performed.

"He completed a few passes, and threw the ball well. I was amazed," he said. "I wasn't sure he could even take a snap. I'd never seen him do that."

There were other glimmers of Alex's inner strength and talent that would prove to be monumental assets later. "I saw the confidence that he knew he could do it," Steve remembered. "He was telling his dad that he'd never played quarterback before, but he knew he could do it."

## SKI PATROL

Sandwiched between three outgoing siblings, Alex developed a shy, quiet personality. He had little use for his vocal cords. Though he now speaks in front of the media throngs with finesse, the skill didn't come naturally.

"Alex was the child who didn't even talk," Doug said. "He had two older siblings who talked plenty for him. Then along came MacKenzie who was extremely verbal. He probably had to go to first grade before he got to speak. His older and younger sisters would speak for him."

This aspect of his relationship with his siblings became abundantly clear one winter day. MacKenzie, Josh and Alex were skiing on the powdery slopes of Park City, Utah. They stopped on the mountain to catch up with one another, unaware that a dangerous situation was about to unfold.

"We all stopped and another skier plowed into Alex and knocked everything off of him: his skis, his poles, his goggles," MacKenzie remembered painfully. "It was a very hard hit onto the packed snow."

Alex was dazed by the crash and suffered a mild concussion. In a lucky twist of fate, the ski patrol happened to be coming down the mountain right after it happened. They began their usual routine of checking out an injured skier to gauge the severity of Alex's head trauma. MacKenzie looked on with worry.

"They asked him, 'Do you know where you are and what you had for breakfast?'" MacKenzie remembered. "I went over to Alex and tapped him on the shoulder and said, 'You're in Park City and you had a muffin for breakfast.'

"I was too young to understand that he'd had a concussion and couldn't remember," MacKenzie laughed. "I was trying to give him the answers. I thought I was doing a favor for him but really I wasn't helping."

MacKenzie said that incident on the mountain summed up their sibling relationship. Alex may be older, but she called the shots.

Likewise, Alex felt an innate responsibility for his exuberant younger sister. He included her in baseball and football games with the neighborhood kids.

"When we'd play basketball in the back yard, even if we were on different teams, he'd always go easy on me," MacKenzie said with a smile. "If I fell, he was there. He was a good brother."

Alex was always kind to everyone, a far cry from the stereotypical image of a football player.

"He was way too nice of a child," Doug said. "He was too nice to play football, too caring. You think of football players as angry, violent, tough guys—Alex isn't any of those things. He's highly focused and he has tenacity. But when you think of the typical qualities in a potential football player, that wasn't Alex."

Doug later told one of his varsity football coaches that he didn't know what kind of football player Alex would be because he was always so kind to others. Now, Doug believes his son's benevolent nature and selflessness are strong assets as an athlete. His ability to think of others first endeared him to the local and national media when he became known as "the humble star athlete who gave the credit for his success to his teammates."

"He doesn't take himself too seriously," Doug explained. "He's not overly self-absorbed. He doesn't have that in him."

## A MESSAGE IN A BAGGIE

Alex learned a valuable lesson about the nature of the news media the day his uncle Ronnie stood near an irrigation ditch on his farmland in Idaho. It was a lovely autumn day. Alex was nine years old and living in San Diego. Ronnie saw a young girl, about Alex's age, with a face full of hope and promise lean down and put something wistfully into the water. Later, while cleaning out the ditch, Ronnie saw a piece of paper float by encased in a Ziploc baggie. It was like a message in a bottle. Inside, the young girl had written a thoughtful letter detailing her life and asking for someone special to write her back. It was a game of chance, an impossible wish. Or was it?

"Ronnie picked the note up because he knew it wouldn't go anywhere," Pam explained. "His ditch emptied into a field."

Ronnie and his wife Susan left for a previously planned visit to see the Smith family in San Diego. Ronnie, ever the jokester, had a plan.

"I threw the note in the suitcase," Ronnie admitted.

An idea hatched easily in his mind. When they arrived in San Diego, Ronnie approached Alex. "I showed him that note and said, 'Here Alex, make this little girl's heart throb.'"

Alex didn't like the idea from the beginning. "Ronnie came

down and said, 'Wouldn't this be funny if you wrote this girl back?' Ever since I can remember I was very shy and not getting in too much trouble" Alex said. "I really hesitated to write the letter. I hoped they'd all forget about it."

Ronnie coaxed Alex, "Why don't you write back and say you found it on the beach in San Diego?"

Alex shrugged off the idea and put it aside. He didn't think any more about it until three months later when Pam found the note again. She encouraged him to humor the girl in Idaho Falls by writing back in good fun. Alex wrote the Idaho girl a reply.

None of them had any idea of the media frenzy that was soon to follow.

"I write the letter to this girl saying I was walking on the beach and I found this letter," Alex explained. "Next thing I learn they believed it and had it all mapped out. All the sudden it's on the news up there and in the newspapers."

Alex received a letter back from the girl that read, "I can't believe you found it." With her note, she included a map of the United States and had traced the path that she thought her message had taken through the canal system to the Snake River to the Columbia River and down the California coast.

Ronnie forgot all about the note he'd given to Alex. Pam called him one day from San Diego and said Alex had sent the letter. At that very instant, Ronnie looked up from his easy chair and his jaw dropped. While talking to Pam, he watched the local TV news station broadcast the lead story about how a message in a baggie washed down the Snake River into the ocean and down the coast to California.

"I wanted it to go away," Ronnie cringed. "The big news got a hold of it about how remarkable it was. It was a little fib just for fun. The news people were calling me and wanted to know where the ditch went. They didn't realize that it went out into my field and went dry."

"But that's about 1,500 miles," Pam quipped. "Plus, Ronnie's ditch went right into the field. It was impossible."

*This is the journey the girl's note would have had to take to make the miraculous voyage from an Idaho field to a San Diego beach.*

Still, the story was big news in Idaho Falls. The *Post Register* ran a front-page story about how a note that was placed in a ditch in Idaho Falls made its way to a beach in San Diego. Local television news reporters picked up the story. One young, zealous reporter stood at a map on a wall and enthusiastically pointed out the Ziploc baggie's impossible journey through canals, waterways and into the ocean. She and other educated journalists and TV news producers were convinced that serendipity had occurred right there in the state best known for its potatoes. *The Associated Press* heard about the piece and flashed a bulletin on their news wire that went to news operations everywhere. The next day, the story was featured in newspapers around the country.

"If anybody had done their homework, they would have seen that if Ronnie's ditch didn't dead-end into the field, the note would've had to go through fifteen dams and hit the Pacific Ocean in Portland," Pam said.

The story became the talk at office water coolers everywhere. Alex's cousin Jenny was sitting in class in Idaho Falls when her teacher pulled down a map and explained to students how the note had traveled. Everybody in the coffee shops were talking about it. Only the wise farmers who knew how the waterways worked were quietly skeptical.

"Everybody thought it would've been a cute thing, and before anything could be straightened out it was this big story," Pam said.

Eventually, the story quietly died. There were no retractions in the newspapers or on television news. "The media didn't quite think through the story," Pam explained. "It was the lead story everyone was talking about, though—how this young girl connected with this young man in San Diego."

Everyone soon forgot about the story except for the little girl, her father and Alex. The dad paid a visit to Ronnie's farm.

Ronnie chuckled, "I told him that it didn't get there in the water but by airplane. He laughed. It was quite a bit of fun."

Alex was cringing back home in San Diego. Pam and Doug had gone out to a restaurant for dinner that night. Fearing a confronting phone call from the girl's father, the two left Alex's older sister with strict instructions.

"They specifically told my sister that if someone calls for Alex, don't let him talk," Alex remembered. "Sure enough, someone calls and Abbey passes me the phone and says, 'Here you go.'"

It was the girl's father on the other end of the line asking him if the story of the note's miraculous journey was true.

"I said it was just a joke and I was sorry," Alex explained. "I met her when we went up to Idaho the next summer. It was pretty awkward. I was so shy and here I'm going to go meet someone I played a trick on."

Eleven years later, Alex would find himself once again in the glare of the media spotlight as a star athlete and Heisman Trophy finalist. Though he felt bad for the young girl, the fortuitous event helped Alex gain shrewd insight into the ups and downs of the news media.

"Before, I believed anything that was printed was fact," he said. "Then I realized, 'Who knows what's true and what's not?'"

# Chapter 3

# HALFTIME AT HELIX HIGH

No one likes to be the new kid at school. Navigating tight cliques and peer groups to find where you fit in can be unnerving. Alex attended Bonita Vista Middle School through the eighth grade. The school was a "true middle school" at the time, schooling students from seventh to ninth grade. Alex left a year early, however, eagerly switching over to Helix Charter High School to start his freshman year where Abbey and Josh had gone to school.

Alex was 5 feet 8 inches tall and weighed only 100 pounds, just a little guy headed into a bold, new world. Helix is a top-notch, powerhouse high school known for its stellar athletes, winning sports teams and strong academics. There are nearly 2,400 students in four grades. Shy and clumsy Alex found his large new school quite daunting.

"It was hard," Alex remembered. "I had really big feet and I was slow. I was the new kid at a new school and I was the principal's son."

With many obstacles ahead of him, Alex searched for a niche to help him fit in.

Jim Arnaiz, assistant athletic director at Helix Charter High School, was the head football coach. The summer before school started Alex was enrolled in an accelerated math course. Arnaiz often saw Alex hanging out in his dad's office after class let out at noon. "He was always on the computer. He was always in there waiting and nagging his dad."

28

## FINDING HIS PLACE

Alex was unsure of what he wanted to delve into next. To fill the time and make friends at Helix, Alex decided to lift weights with the football team after class. "Football was good because it gave me something to identify with at school," he said.

That autumn, Alex played freshman football. "He surely was not one of our bigger, stronger freshman athletes," Arnaiz said.

Looking back, another one of his coaches recognized something unique in Alex—an ability to be resilient—that would serve him well later as a college player.

"After we had some practice, I told Doug that Alex was really tough," said Robert Berg, Alex's assistant defensive line coach at Helix. "In practice, he was getting hit but he always got up with that same goofy smile on his face. Nothing fazed him."

At the time, no one realized the bright future Alex had ahead of him as an athlete, not even his father. One day after another frustrating practice, Berg listened attentively to Doug's suggestions.

Berg recounted an exchange with Alex's father. "Doug said, 'He's a great kid and a smart kid. He's got everything. But he's not a football player. My advice to him was cross country.'"

Alex kept the far-off dream of becoming a college football player tucked close to his heart. He continued to struggle his freshman year in practices and at games. He was a slow, average quarterback back then, but his positive attitude shined through.

"Every practice and game, it didn't matter. Nothing fazed him. He was having fun," Berg said. "He was just tough."

Alex improved each game and worked his way up to being the leader of the freshman team. "In some situations that could be tough because he was the principal's son," Berg explained. "No one ever questioned it. It was obvious he was the most qualified for that position."

But Alex remembered it differently. Just as he was finding his place as a student athlete at Helix, doubts from others followed

*Alex at age 14, posing for his freshman football photo.*

him like a tenacious defensive lineman. His peers claimed he was receiving favoritism.

"I was always told I was just playing because I was the principal's son," Alex said. "Even my sophomore year, I was always told the same thing by everybody, players and students. I would hear it from all different places."

Alex learned to mold his hurt feelings on the football field into something productive and stronger.

"It was hard. It affected me. I was doing so much academically that I didn't have time to lift weights," Alex admitted. "I was a little guy. It really motivated me, especially as I moved onto my senior year. It absolutely motivated me. I knew deep down that I could play."

Alex became best friends with David Edwards, a bright student he had met in honors chemistry. Edwards didn't play football at all. While Edwards was his academic equal, he still marveled at how easily Alex learned chemistry. Something clicked with Alex in chemistry class just as surely as water is two parts hydrogen and one part oxygen. "He never read the book once," said Edwards, who will soon graduate in political science from UCLA. "I don't ever remember him opening the book. He got an A on almost every test."

But Alex had to work much harder at football. Edwards admired Alex's strong work ethics. "I would be sleeping in during the summer and he'd go work out early in the morning at the Helix gym," Edwards said. "He knew he had to put the effort forth to accomplish his goals. He was lifting and throwing just to get better."

In the tenth grade, Alex played quarterback on the junior varsity team, which consisted mostly of sophomore players. He continued to show improvement.

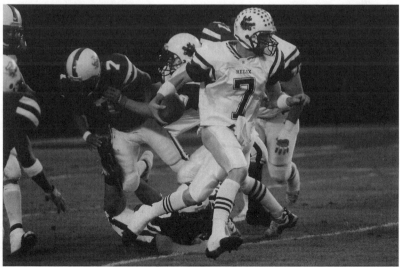

*Alex makes a play as quarterback for Helix High School.*

Alex's sweat and strain yielded fine results. Doug watched his son muster confidence as quarterback. "He was gaining strength. He didn't have his growth spurt yet, but he showed good leadership and a good command of what it meant to be a quarterback," Doug said. "He was developing a pretty good arm at that point."

Arnaiz too began to see the inklings of a future champion quarterback. "You could see he had good decision-making skills," he said. "He was well-liked and well-respected, which are many of the things you needed to have to be a good quarterback. I had no idea he'd develop to the extent that he did. You could see Alex was going to be a good quarterback—how good, nobody really knew."

Along with his hard work at practice, Alex focused on his studies and took advanced placement college courses on top of his regular course load. It's a feat that later allowed him to begin at the University of Utah as a junior.

Alex took AP European History his sophomore year. Ben Stone was his teacher. "He got really good grades in the class and participated all the time," Stone said. "He had a positive outlook." Though Alex didn't pass his first AP exam, he worked hard and received an A at the end of the semester, demonstrating the trademark resiliency that would be another asset on the football field. Stone said Alex was "a levelheaded guy who was nice to everyone," students and teachers alike.

Years later, before the 2004 football season began, Alex sent a signed University of Utah football poster to Stone that read, "Hey Mr. Stone, when was the Battle of Hastings? Ha, Ha. Thank you for everything you taught me." It's a keepsake Stone cherishes. (The answer, by the way, is: the year 1066 when the French invaded England.)

For Alex, studying came before football—not the other way around. "I always told him to focus on the academic side," Stone said. "He's a success story beyond the sports aspect. He went in as a good football player and a top-notch student as well."

## THE ALEX-MOBILE

When Alex turned 16, his dad took him car shopping. Most guys his age dream of driving a red convertible to school each day, or they practically salivate over the idea of driving a sleek and sporty SUV. Many teenage boys can almost picture themselves picking up a hot date with the sunroof opened. But Doug had other plans for his son.

"We wanted a vehicle that didn't carry very many people," Doug said. "It's important for teenagers to not have a car where they can drive a lot of other kids around, for safety reasons."

Doug also wanted to teach Alex his first lesson in economics: cars are not good investments. It may have also been his very first tutorial in humility. Doug bought him a 1982 Toyota pick-up truck that had more rust on the body than paint. You could hardly tell the truck was once a fine shade of fire engine red, but it functioned well and only cost $800.

"You deliver any kind of vehicle to a teenage boy and it goes downhill from there," Doug said. And it did. After Alex drove it for a while, the windows wouldn't roll up or down, the interior was torn, and it had a few more dents on its rusty exterior.

MacKenzie often rode to school with Alex. "During the rainy season it would leak a lot," she recalled with a laugh.

The passenger door wouldn't open, so every morning she had to climb through the driver's side door to get in. The radio didn't work so he kept a boom box inside. The bumper was only three inches from the ground and scraped the pavement when he went over speed bumps.

Alex soon experienced a growth spurt, and the small truck became a tight squeeze for him. "Sometimes he gave a couple football players a ride home and they'd fill up the truck pretty fast," MacKenzie said.

But one thing was crystal clear—people always knew when Alex Smith rounded a corner. "He was famous for that vehicle," Doug recalled. "Necks would turn and people would see that truck coming and say, 'Whoa, that's bad.'"

The truck was symbolic of Alex's personality—no flash, just genuine dependability. That's how he soon learned to play football. "He's got the arm and the speed. He just gets it done," MacKenzie said. "You can always count on him and he always comes through."

## WINNING HIS FIRST CHAMPIONSHIP

During his junior year, Alex had shot up in height to six feet three inches tall.

Doug said, "Though he was quite thin, he now had the height in terms of throwing quarterbacks that you desire. He continued to develop in terms of his arm and his leadership on the field."

Gordon Wood, dean of students at Terracotta Middle School, was the head varsity coach at Helix and the quarterbacks coach. He didn't know Alex during his freshman and sophomore seasons and never saw him struggle. Because of this, he had more confidence in him as a player. When Wood first met him, Alex had already matured on and off the football field.

*Alex makes a nice gain for Helix High through several defenders.*

"I could see some skills developing," Wood said.

In an interesting twist of fate, Doug had been Wood's football coach in high school and was now his boss at Helix. Yet, despite their close ties, Doug made it clear to Wood that he didn't want any preferential treatment for Alex. "He said, 'Just because you're the head coach and he's my son doesn't mean he's the guy for the job of varsity quarterback.'"

Immediately, Wood saw beyond Alex's cool focus and recognized his courage. "He's not afraid to be put into positions where you depend on him," he explained. "You find out a lot about student athletes when you put them in an arena when it's not so easy. A lot of kids can compete when there's not a lot of pressure. When you throw 'em in the fire, either they're going to run or step up to the challenges. He steps up to the challenges. He doesn't just get lucky. He prepares himself mentally and physically."

Alex would dissect the game in his mind, carefully studying plays and seeking to understand the game. "He wants to know the complete picture," Wood explained.

He played varsity quarterback with a talented team, including running back Reggie Bush, who later became a star at the University of Southern California and a Heisman Trophy finalist. With the winning combination of Alex's cool efficiency and Reggie's swiftness, the team went undefeated. That year, they beat out 80 other high schools to win the San Diego Interscholastic Federation Championship, California's equivalent to the state football championship.

Even as Alex began to blossom as a quarterback, the prospect of playing beyond high school still seemed way out of his grasp. "If someone had told me I was college prospect, I would've said to you that they were lying. It seemed so far off. Recruiters came in the spring asking about Reggie. The recruiters were asking, 'What about your quarterback?' I was shocked. Just like I was shocked when the NFL wanted me. I was so excited. It was deep down a dream to play college football. It drove me to make huge strides during my senior year."

Mimi Test, assistant principal at Helix and a close friend of the Smith family, was also a beloved veteran coach. She was the first woman in San Diego County to coach a boys swim team, leading them to 149 wins and only one loss.

"One of the most authentic classrooms you can have is the athletic venue, whether it's a court or a swimming pool," Test explained. "Coaches get into the hearts and souls of kids. You can produce great results, but you have to get into the hearts of kids to get phenomenal results."

Test noticed how Alex's tenacity grew into a strength, just like the rest of his body began to grow and catch up with his big feet. "In between his junior and senior year he just shot up," she remembered. "His natural skills became noticeable talents. He didn't walk into Helix with those skills developed. He went through a process during those three or four years of making a conscious choice to put in the effort. That's what separates him from other athletes."

Alex's passion for the game drove him to become the very best player on the field.

"He's a Cinderella story of effort, determination, opportunity and choice," Test said. "He made the conscious choice to make the greatest of all efforts. Some athletes come in with talent and rely on talent to showcase their efforts."

## WINNING A SECOND CHAMPIONSHIP

Alex was growing more confident in practice every day. That fall of his senior year, he continued being a student of the game. Every week, he'd inquisitively walk into his coaches' offices and drill them with the same questions each Monday and Tuesday. By the Wednesday before the game, Alex would sometimes feel extremely frustrated.

"He wanted to know what we were going to try to accomplish," Wood said. "He'd ask, 'What's the game plan?'"

Each Thursday, the coaches did a walk-through with the team and they would finalize the plan for the upcoming game. Alex would literally play the game in his head. In his mind, he'd visualize plays to see if they would really work. While assessing the situation, he'd make mental adjustments for the game ahead of him.

Such intense study allowed him to develop an uncanny ability to be in tune with the coaches. "He is a coach on the field in the way that you hope that he is," Wood said. "He tried to become in unison with the coach on the field. He'd be making a suggestion and he'd be saying almost what the coach was going to say to him at the same time."

His coaches gained so much confidence in Alex that they developed "the Christmas series," a group of plays that gave him the full authority to run the offense. Alex called the plays and made the decisions. "It was like saying, 'Let's see how he handles this situation,'" Wood remembered. "Most kids would go for the gusto and make big plays. He did it in the way he was taught to do it—very responsibly. He'd run plays in sequence and in the way the coach was trying to teach him. He was patient. It's reflective on the way he plays now."

It worked. The team lost only one game and won the championship for the second year in a row. The school had won the football championship only three other times in its 50-year history.

Doug watched his son revel in success as the momentum grew. "As you march forward in that process and the tournament, it's a big deal. The media pays more and more attention to it," Doug said. "It becomes a major event for your school. As a parent, it becomes a very significant accomplishment. Championships don't happen all that often. To win it twice in a row was amazing."

Alex had believed Reggie was responsible for winning the championship the year before. His senior year, he finally began to appreciate his own contributions to the team and took ownership for his emerging abilities. "I felt like I was much more of a direct cause. We still had Reggie, but I felt like a lot more of it was on my shoulders. And I liked it."

*Alex and his dad Doug celebrate Helix High's second straight CIF championship.*

He also began to navigate the tightrope that quarterbacks walk between having moxie and being realistic.

"I learned that when I forced things and tried too hard, that's when I didn't play well," Alex explained. "You can't think about winning the game with every pass. You can't think, 'This is a big game, I've got to throw for 300 yards.' In fact, you've got to play the way that got you there. You can't press things."

Josh had graduated from UC Davis and was back living in San Diego. The close proximity enabled him to attend each game, including the championship. "It was a lot like the Fiesta Bowl but on a much smaller scale," Josh remembered. "He was Player of the Game."

Even as Alex became the big man on campus, his devotion to his family never swayed. During an interview, a local television reporter asked him, "Who's your biggest hero?" His answer wasn't a big time NFL player who had won the Super Bowl. Alex's response was, "My dad."

Despite his busy schedule, Alex still always had time for MacKenzie. "When I came to campus, he was never embarrassed to hang out with his younger sister," she said. "He always included me, introduced me to all of his friends and let me be friends with them. He never told me hang out somewhere else."

At halftime of the Homecoming game his senior year Helix, Alex was crowned king. His mom celebrated the happy moment with him and escorted him down the aisle. The reserved kid who transferred from junior high had found his niche.

"Alex is such a nice person," Pam said. "He's so likable. I never hear him say a bad word about anybody. He was senior class president, homecoming king, and the star quarterback because the other kids just loved him. He was never full of himself. He was always kind and sweet. That's genuine. That's who Alex is."

*The King and Queen stand before the crowd.*

*Alex with his mom after being crowned Homecoming King during a halftime ceremony.*

*The Homecoming Court at Helix High School, where Alex was crowned Homecoming King during his senior year.*

*Alex with his mom before the high school Senior Prom.*

*Alex with his dad Doug and sisters Abbey (on Alex's back) and MacKenzie.*

## THE ARTISTIC ATHLETE

Alex sharpened his artistic talents that year and gained a close friendship in the process. Jane Huntington, an 83-year-old artist who owned her own gallery in Chula Vista, taught him art lessons on Saturdays. She set up card tables and tubes of paint in bright hues of orange, chocolate and emerald, along with paintbrushes of varying sizes to teach Alex all the knowledge she had gained from a lifetime of painting.

"I told him that the best thing you can do is to paint what comes naturally," she said.

During one assignment, Huntington asked Alex to bring a picture of "something that really grabs you." Alex brought a photo of a picturesque mountain scene in Big Sky, Montana, where the family was building a vacation condo. Such a scene is one of the hardest landscapes to paint, but by the time he had finished smoothing his brush over the canvas, the painting was so good that his mom thought his teacher had painted it. Huntington recognized his natural artistic talent.

"I thought, 'This kid's really got it,'" Huntington remembered. "You just have to feel it. You have an instinct for the colors. You can look at something and know what colors to mix. It's like people

*Alex and Jane Huntington, his friend and art teacher. Alex has developed into a talented artist. Below, Alex carefully touches up a painting.*

who are good at cooking who don't always get it out of a book. They have a feel. I let him do his own thing. That was the answer."

## THE FOOTBALL PLAYER TO BE

Was it a prophetic moment in the classroom? Or, was it just a creative way for a teacher to teach economics? The day Gifford Asimos, economics teacher at Helix, chose to use football as an allegory for his AP Micro and Macro Economics class, will always stand out in his memory. Asimos asked for a volunteer from the class to role-play a principle. Alex raised his hand and volunteered, just like he always did. The lesson that day was about the Federal Reserve and how it makes adjustments to the economy. "I was trying to get through to the students that there's a time lag from when the Fed takes action. It's six to eight months until it's felt in the economy," Asimos explained.

*Alex with teammate Reggie Bush at the Helix High football awards banquet following their senior season. Less than three years later, these two friends would be Heisman Trophy finalists together.*

The teacher picked up a Nerf football. Alex was sitting in the back of the crowded classroom. Asimos tossed him the football then asked him stand up and throw him a pass. "I started like I was going to run, and Alex threw the pass. Right when he threw it I stopped. The pass hit the floor six feet in front of me. I asked Alex, 'What was the problem? Why didn't you make the pass here?'"

Alex answered, "I anticipated that you'd keep running."

The teacher explained that the Federal Reserve, like a quarterback, has to think ahead. The validity or foolishness of a quarterback's decisions might not become apparent until the end of the game, just as the Feds' actions don't register in the economy for six to nine months down the road. "They have to think about where the economy's going to be in six to nine months," Asimos said. "I think the class got it."

Alex got it too. Later, as quarterback at the University of Utah, he became known by sports writers and pundits for his ability to make wise split-second decisions that assured a win.

"He's constantly thinking, trying to anticipate what's going to happen and reacting to that," Asimos said. "It has helped him in his football career, absolutely."

Another moment of foresight happened one afternoon after his senior football season was finished. Alex was playing football with his best friend David and another friend, Andre. Alex instructed Andre to run a hook pattern for ten or fifteen yards. Instead, Andre ran in a half circle pattern instead of a tighter route like Alex had asked him. He didn't stick to the play. "Alex threw the ball, a line drive and it whizzed past my face and hit Andre squarely in the nose and almost knocked him out," David said. "It was a testament to Alex's arm strength. No one knew his potential at that point, but I always knew he'd do well."

Even with two championships under his belt, Alex remained relatively underrated, overshadowed by the acclaimed running back Reggie Bush. Most of the time, Alex didn't even have to throw the ball. He'd simply hand off to Reggie who would run it into the end zone. The plays were successful, but Alex didn't get a chance to prove he had a strong arm along with gifted, precise focus.

Pam stood in the stands with the rest of the family cheering him on, but inside she knew that he could do more than was readily apparent. "Alex would be out by halftime because they were winning by so much and the coaches didn't want to run up the score," Pam said.

For these reasons, Alex didn't have the impressive statistics in high school that other quarterbacks did. Many steely-eyed recruiters passed him by—a decision they would come to regret.

# Chapter 4

# THE DECISION TO
# GO TO UTAH

Alex felt the heaviness of the choice of where to go to college like a weighty backpack full of textbooks. So much hinged on this decision—his future as an athlete, his potential as a scholar and the next turn his life would take. He faced a kaleidoscope of possibilities.

The Ivy League schools were courting him. The chance to attend Harvard, the University of Pennsylvania, or Princeton was well within his reach. Pam thought the opportunity to attend such a prestigious school was too good to pass up. "I thought, 'What a great chance to go to Harvard or Penn,'" Pam said. "I tried to talk him into that."

But Alex couldn't let go of the dream he had when he was a little boy who liked to play football in the backyard with his older brother. "It was quite an opportunity to go to Harvard, Dartmouth or Princeton," Alex said. "But because college football was in my family and in my blood I wasn't going to let that opportunity pass me by. I wanted to play Division 1-A football and find out how good I was."

## CONSIDERING LOUISVILLE

There was also another college option. His uncle John L. Smith was then the head football coach at the University of Louisville, a perennial bowl team that had sent many players to the NFL. Louisville was interested in Alex, but Alex was naturally wary of how others would view the family connection.

"It shouldn't make a difference whether or not I'm here," John assured him, torn between his responsibilities as football coach and his unconditional love for his brother's son. "We're not recruiting you because you're my nephew. Don't make the decision because I'm your uncle. When you make the decision, you do what's right for you. Your heart will tell you the right place."

Louisville seemed an appealing choice. He looked up to his uncle with affection. He liked how the Louisville offense operated. Having a father figure like his uncle to guide him through the pitfalls of Division 1-A football would ease his nerves. Perhaps John would make the transition from playing in high school to the rough world of college football go a little more smoothly.

His parents agreed. "To have a resource, a family member, in that situation, presented an opportunity for Alex," Doug said.

With his father's blessing, Alex believed Louisville would be the right place for him. "That was his first choice, clearly. You couldn't have asked for anything better," Doug explained. "When your kids

*Alex and his family at his high school graduation in June 2002.*

go off to play football at the college level, you wonder how they'll be treated. College is big business at the Division 1-A level. A lot of things happen that don't put the athlete first. You have concerns about those schools that are recruiting your child. I knew full well that I trusted my brother with my son, to do the best for him."

While most other colleges in Division 1-A didn't even give Alex so much as a glance, he continued to believe in himself. "I wasn't a huge recruit at the time, but I felt like I could play," he said.

John, however, was well aware of Alex's hidden talents. He had kept a watchful eye on his nephew over the years. He had traveled to San Diego to watch Alex play in the state semifinal game his junior year. He noticed Alex's athletic ability was getting sharper after winning the championship that same year. "John followed him very closely after that," Doug said.

John remembered, "All the sudden he was throwing the ball. He got better and better all the time. I knew he was smart, a decent height and had a good arm on him. The thing I liked best about him was his accuracy and intelligence in knowing who to throw the ball to. My least favorite thing about him was his feet. I thought we were going to have to get him to be a lot quicker."

## A DIAMOND IN THE ROUGH

Only one other school with a Division 1-A football team was even interested in him—the University of Utah. Defensive backs coach Bill Busch recognized raw athletic potential when he saw it, and he saw Alex as a brassy, old trophy hidden in a closet just waiting for a good shine.

"I give him 100 percent credit that Alex got a scholarship at Utah," Pam said.

Busch believed Alex was something special. That belief was the impetus for all the magic and groundbreaking achievements that would follow.

"I'd seen him work out before. I just knew we had to get someone to see him," said Busch, who recruited the Southern California area for the Utes at the time, and is now the outside linebacker coach and special teams coordinator at the University of Nebraska.

"I knew going into it we weren't going to see a ton a film on him," Busch remembered. "His team was so successful that there were a lot times he didn't play in the second half."

Busch was looking at five other recruits in California at the time. On paper, Alex was a weak candidate. He was tall and skinny, a lightweight who also played for the golf team. Yes, he was smart and played quarterback for a championship team, but could he even throw the football?

"I needed someone to see his talents, because when he walked in the door he wasn't intimidating," Busch explained.

Back at Helix, Coach Wood encouraged Busch to keep Alex in mind. He told Busch, "Bill, you have no idea what you've got."

Busch continued to follow Alex's career, and he soon marveled at Alex's potential. Alex rarely threw an incomplete pass during his senior year at Helix. Plus, Busch was immediately taken with Alex's parents. He liked their easy-going, friendly personalities and sound parental judgments.

"Doug and Pam totally understood how football works," he recalled. "At home, he was being told, 'Go to college, get good grades and work hard at it,' rather than an emphasis on reaching the NFL. He wasn't treated like a prodigy. He was a normal kid. Alex was so grounded."

All these qualities, he believed, added up to promise not yet realized. "I'm smart enough to know when I see a great player," Busch said.

Busch picked up the phone and called Utah offensive coordinator Craig Ver Steeg, pleading with him to take a good look at this relatively unknown high school player. "You gotta see this kid throw," he said. "He's special. He has the skills no one else has."

Busch reasoned with Ver Steeg that because Alex didn't have the impressive numbers, Utah would be getting a bargain. "He was a little under the radar so we had a chance to get him," Busch recalled.

Ver Steeg traveled to San Diego. On a slick, wet day at Helix High, Alex walked calmly and nonchalantly onto the football field as if it were just another day of practice. Ver Steeg watched with intense concentration while this small-time player demonstrated his remarkable arm strength and accuracy. "Craig was impressed," Busch said, and a recruiting visit for Alex was scheduled.

## A TRIP TO UTAH

Busch brought Alex to Utah to show him the university. It was only a short 90-minute flight to Salt Lake City from San Diego, compared to the full day and evening of traveling by airplane across the country to Louisville. Alex liked the close proximity to his hometown. Plus, he had always been drawn to the outdoors. The splendor and beauty of the Wasatch Mountains evoked fond memories of the ski trips he had taken to Park City with his family. It immediately felt familiar. Alex was starting to feel at home.

Busch accentuated the positive aspects of coming to Utah as best as he could. He reasoned with Alex that with family close by, he would have the support system he needed. Busch knew how important family was to his recruit. On that fateful recruiting trip, he and Busch became friends. Busch remembered, "A lot of times we sat and talked, not even about football."

Busch treated Alex like the star player he thought he could be, even while other schools scoffed at such a soft recruit. "I knew what a special player we had from the start," he quipped. "The bigger schools talked down a little about him like, 'Oh, he'll be a good player for *you.*'"

While the decision between Utah and Louisville had been neck-and-neck before, by the time Alex returned, his choice was becoming clear. "Utah recruited me so hard. They wanted me so much," he said.

Abbey said, "I remember him going on both of the recruiting trips and there was a little different feel when he came back from Utah. The family was closer, and there was a big draw to the outdoors and the mountains. He came home excited."

Doug was pleased with the recent improvements at the Utah athletic facilities. He also believed his son would get a better education there rather than at Louisville. "It was clearly the strongest academic school," he said.

## THE DECISION

Utah and Louisville both offered Alex scholarships. It was time to make a decision.

Doug warned Alex against having a myopic view. "You want to make sure you're making it for a whole series of right decisions," Doug told him.

He also reminded his son that he needed to keep his emphasis on academics rather than football. "You're going off to get a college degree and play college football. Beyond that, there's no guarantee. You're going to get a degree from the best university you can, then move on to a strong graduate program."

Another factor continued to pester Alex like an old wound. Would anyone take his scholarship to Louisville seriously? Or would they cry nepotism the same way his peers did during his freshman year at Helix?

"I questioned why Louisville was recruiting me," Alex admitted. "Was he just recruiting me because he was my uncle?"

John, too, felt conflicted about coaching his nephew. Would Louisville be the best choice for Alex? "I would've liked to have coached him," he said. "At the same point, you look at him and say, 'This is my nephew. I want him to do what's best for him.' I would've been the only support system for him here. That might've been awkward. Maybe I would've been tougher on him or too lenient. Typically dads who are coaches have trouble coaching their own kids."

Josh weighed in on the choice as Alex's protective, older brother. "I knew that by going to Louisville people could always say, 'He's just there for John. This is a family-offered scholarship.' It was good to see him make his own name," he said.

Doug worried about the drawbacks of having his brother coach

Alex as well. "If Alex were to have gone there and done well, would people have asked, 'Is it just because his uncle's the head coach?' The family thing can be a drawback. It certainly was Alex's first choice, though, if everything else would've been right."

Besides, other head coaching opportunities were brewing for John. There is never a guarantee that a head coach will remain at a university when a player signs on. John made it clear to Alex his time at Louisville was tentative.

In fact, John soon left and became the head coach at Michigan State, where he continues his illustrious career. John has led six teams to bowl games, racked up 110 career wins and produced six conference championships.

Alex said, "When John told me he probably wasn't going to be there, it made the decision easier. Utah was an easy choice in the end."

Alex accepted the scholarship to Utah just before Christmas of 2001. Then on Christmas day Utah beat USC in the Las Vegas Bowl. "He got a chance to see that game," Busch said. "It solidified what we were already doing with him."

Utah now seemed to be the right choice. "He liked the academics of Utah," Pam said. "He loved the area. He thought there was going to be a good opportunity for him to play and get in there as quarterback. He knew it was a fine institution. Alex was thrilled."

John was gracious about Alex's choice. "I thought it was great school," John explained. "I was proud of the kid for going there. Had he been my son, I would've told him that was my choice. He had the support system of family close by."

Alex's dream was coming true. That characteristic grin of his was growing wider. The little boy in him was ecstatic. "Utah seemed to fit with everything," Alex said.

Still, Alex never imagined that going to Utah was only the beginning of his phenomenal college career that would take Utah to new heights and catapult him to the NFL, one of the few players whose dream of playing pro football actually comes true.

In retrospect, even Bill Busch hadn't a clue of the athletic wonder he had helped sign. "The plan was to be a great quarterback at Utah," he reflected. "The NFL draft was never a topic of conversation with us."

# Chapter 5

# THROWN INTO THE FIRE

Even though most college football recruiters had given Alex a complacent yawn, the clumsy kid from San Diego had received the opportunity that he needed. Sometimes, it takes just one person believing in you. Alex found that individual in Bill Busch, who saw a spark in Alex that was about to ignite.

That summer, Alex headed to preseason camp in Salt Lake City. It appeared everything was going exactly as he'd dreamed.

## A DISAPPOINTING YEAR

However, when Alex arrived he encountered obstacles he couldn't have foreseen. He found that the coaching staff was a bit lackadaisical and some of his teammates complained constantly at workouts. The result was a team devoid of passion. "Everybody whined about practice, and the coaches didn't have a lot of energy. It was very businesslike," Alex said. "I had dreamed about what it would be like for so long and it was the exact opposite."

It didn't take long for Alex and his parents to separate the dream of his college football experience from the harsh reality. Pam said, "It was a very hard year. You watch your kids go off to achieve a dream. He had a chance to go to Harvard, Princeton or Penn but he wanted to play Division 1-A football."

The emotional wounds from that disastrous first year still sting today. Arguably, no future starting quarterback had a rougher beginning at the University of Utah than Alex Smith.

## WARMING UP

Before the 2002 season began, Alex wowed his teammates with his gusto at preseason camp and games. His enthusiasm and keen arm strength made others take note. "He really impressed everyone at the first scrimmage in the fall," said Tommy Hackenbruck, Utah inside linebacker who graduated in business finance. "He went in with the backups and was moving the ball down the field. Everyone was saying, 'Dang, this kid's going to be good. He's got a good arm.'"

To his coaches, Alex was just another tall, gangly athlete fresh out of high school. But Kyle Whittingham remembered how other qualities made Alex stand out like the Ugly Duckling. "You could tell from the get-go that he had something special—intelligence, character and maturity that very few freshmen possess," he said.

These same traits that made Alex unique as a freshman player later grew into the wings that helped him to soar athletically. "Those skills are invaluable," Whittingham explained. "As good as he is physically, what sets him apart from the other guys is the way he can run the ball and execute. He has the physical talent and the decision-making skills. His field awareness is the best I've seen in my life."

Yet, these assets weren't enough to propel Alex ahead of more seasoned players. That fall, Alex sat on the bench as a third-string quarterback behind two talented leaders: Brett Elliot and Lance Rice. Never the pushy parents, Pam and Doug gladly accepted their son's situation. They had no expectations that he would even get to play his freshman year. They viewed it as a time for him to dip his toe in the tepid water and learn what college football was about. They wanted him to take it slowly.

"We were fine with him redshirting. We thought that was a good decision," Pam recalled. "There were two quarterbacks ahead of him. It's what we wanted. They told us they were going to have him dressing on the sidelines to gain the experience of being on the sidelines and being there."

## A PROPHETIC STATEMENT

Even though they knew their son wouldn't get to play his freshman year, Pam and Doug still attended that very first game against Utah State in Logan. They wanted to show Alex some moral support and help build his confidence. Plus, they'd be able to spend a little time with him over the Labor Day weekend.

Eagerly, they headed to the USU campus for the season opener. Having never met head coach Ron McBride's wife, Vicky, the fact that they were sitting right next to her in the stadium went unnoticed. Before the game began, they struck up conversations with other players' parents. While chatting with them they realized they were sitting next to the head coach's wife. They introduced themselves.

"Once she learned who we were, she went out of her way to tell us how much she liked Alex," Doug remembered. "We appreciated hearing that."

What Vicky said next to Pam and Doug was either clairvoyant or an amazingly good guess. Her foresight was uncanny. "She said that Alex was going to be the best quarterback in Utah history," Doug remembered. "She had a prophetic prediction of his accomplishments. He hadn't played a down yet. I remember thinking, 'That was nice of her to say.'"

## LOSING HIS REDSHIRT YEAR

The Utes, led by McBride, a well-liked veteran coach, expected to have a strong season. The team was coming off a Las Vegas Bowl victory and the media picked them to be among the best teams in the Mountain West Conference.

In that season opener at Logan, the Utes beat Utah State 23-3. Then in their first home game they toppled Indiana 40-13.

Their good fortune was short-lived, however. They next played at Arizona and lost 23-17. That disappointment was followed by a 10-7 loss to Michigan and a 30-26 defeat against Air Force. Suddenly the Utes were 2-3 and starting to unravel.

That's when Pam and Doug received some news that unnerved them. "We're nearly halfway through the season and we get a call that they're considering going with Alex, or 'shared 50-50 time,'" Pam remembered.

Along with having been a football coach, Doug also played college football at Weber State University. He knew as a former player that if you're going to be taken off the bench and lose a year of eligibility, it needs to be worth your while. Doug talked to offensive coordinator Craig Ver Steeg and asked him, "If you're going to pull him out of his redshirt, you wouldn't do that to have him be a back-up, would you?" Doug said Ver Steeg told him Alex would either be the starter or play a lot.

Doug and Pam exhaled after being assured that Alex would only be pulled out of his redshirt year if he was going to play. He wouldn't be the starter, but the plan was to give him some playing time in each game.

His debut would be in front of his hometown crowd when Utah played San Diego State. Hundreds of people attended the game to cheer him on, including his family, his old coaches, teachers and friends. The pressure to perform well was high. This was his chance to showcase his talent to all the peers who had doubted him in high school, and he could make his family proud. He could also help end the Utes' three-game losing streak. Alex didn't want to let anyone down.

Pam and Doug were nervous for their son, and they grew more edgy as the game progressed. After taking an early lead, the Utes allowed the Aztecs to pull way ahead. Alex remained on the bench. "Surely they won't put him in now," Doug thought.

As the third quarter began, Doug saw something that disturbed him. After receiving instructions from his coaches, Alex was on the sideline throwing the ball to warm up. Utah was in bad field position and losing handily. His son had never stepped onto the turf at a college game before in his life.

Doug knew that not even a seasoned player could pull off the miracle that the Utes needed to come from behind and win. But a third-string quarterback who had zero college game experience? No way. Were they really going to put Alex in under these circumstances?

Intuitively, Doug knew that the answer was a resounding yes. "I was in disbelief," Doug recalled. "Not just as his father, but as a person who knows a little about coaching kids. That you'd put a player on the field at quarterback for the first time in that situation was ridiculous."

Sure enough, Coach McBride called Brett Elliot off the field. Alex was about to begin his college football career. The moment he stepped onto the field he would sacrifice a year of eligibility. Pam said wryly, "Utah's getting beaten badly. They're in a terrible field position. They all of the sudden put Alex in when the dam's breaking. It isn't what you do with a young kid developing. It's like throwing him into the deep end of the swimming pool."

Alex played for only two series and five plays. In the first series, Alex started off with a short completion, but then he was sacked twice, and the Utes were forced to punt. On the following series, Alex started deep in his own territory and completed a five-yard pass. On the next play the Aztecs' Ricky Sharpe intercepted Alex's pass and returned it 29 yards for a touchdown.

It would have been difficult to have a worse beginning. Alex's college debut yielded minus 11 yards rushing and a touchdown for the other team. Alex was humiliated in front of his family and his hometown crowd. Coach McBride took him out of the game immediately. Alex walked off the field dazed and discouraged.

"I will never forget him coming off the field. Your heart is just aching," Pam said. "This is his dream in front of his hometown. They couldn't have picked a worse situation. They set him up to fail. His redshirt year is blown."

Doug's blood was boiling. He had placed his faith in the coaches to do what was best for his son and they let him down. "You never put a player in for the first time like that. No coach in America would tell you that was a good thing to do."

Doug had long been an advocate of positive reinforcement as

a coach and principal. He knew that Alex, like any athlete, had to believe in himself in order to have a chance at success. Doug believed coaches should only play young, inexperienced players when the circumstances were ripe for accomplishment, not the other way around.

"You don't create an impossible situation and tell them to go in and play with confidence," he explained. "You might start the game with him, or put him in at the start of the second half. That would give him an opportunity to have success. What they did then was terrible. It guaranteed no success."

Family and friends felt deep empathy for Alex. They couldn't believe his first chance playing college football had gone so poorly.

His teammates felt bad for him too. "I knew he was in front of his home crowd," Hackenbruck recalled. "I watched Brett Elliot struggle and then they put Alex in. We were already trailing and playing horribly. Even our defense was playing horribly. I felt horrible after he threw that interception and he lost his redshirt year. He was put in such a tough situation."

Winning has its place. So does standing back up, dusting the dirt of your knees and trying again. But Alex didn't get a chance to play again for the rest of the game. The coaches made him sit on the bench and all he could do was reflect upon his performance. His parents believed he deserved a chance to redeem himself and show he could be resilient.

Doug added, "They didn't continue to play him or say, 'This game is already over. You're going to go out there and keep playing because you're going to get better.' They didn't do that."

Not letting him play again in the game irked the Smiths more than the coaches' hasty decision to throw him into the fire. "The game was already gone," Doug explained. "You should've known it wasn't likely to happen. So what? Put him back in again. At least let him get more than five plays in."

Alex winced at the memory. "It was difficult. I had done so well in practice. I think that's why they pulled me off the redshirt. It was hard to take. I thought I could play by that point. I'd gone through half a year of practice. It was so disappointing how everything was handled off the field."

The disastrous game was Utah's fourth straight loss. The losing streak wasn't over yet. After that fateful game, Colorado State beat Utah 28-20 on their home turf at Rice-Eccles Stadium.

Having lost his redshirt year, Alex wanted to make the most of the situation. He expected to gain vital playing experience on the field in the remainder of the games. But the coaches made promises they didn't keep. Every week before the game, Alex said that his coaches told him he'd get the opportunity to play. Alex passed that information along to his parents. So, Pam and Doug traveled to every game. Each time, they left disappointed.

Pam remembered, "It was discouraging sitting in those stands, knowing Alex had worked hard all week, then waiting for him to go back in and prove himself. Then he never got that opportunity. Week after week we went up there. The coaching staff was on the verge of getting fired and scrambling to save their jobs."

The next game was against New Mexico. The coaches finally put Alex in the game again. Alex threw an incomplete pass. Immediately the coaches yanked him out again and put him back on the bench. He got to play only one snap of the ball. Pam was baffled. "What sense does one play make?"

The game ended in another disappointing loss for the Utes. That game would mark the only other time Alex stepped onto the field to play that whole season.

Alex said, "I got lied to the rest of the year. I was very disappointed with my college football experience at that point."

Utah went on to win against UNLV, Wyoming and in-state rival Brigham Young University. But the damage was already done. The season had been a flop and Alex lost a year of eligibility.

While Busch, who brought Alex to Utah, didn't make the decision to have Alex play against San Diego State, he still wanted to make amends. He called Alex into his office and apologized. He explained to Alex how much he regretted the coaches' decision to play him in a disastrous attempt to salvage that game.

"In hindsight, [putting him in] was a bad choice," Busch explained. "He was put in a no-win situation late in the game."

Chris Hill, who has been the Utes' athletic director for nearly two decades, agreed.

"I felt very bad about that," Hill said. "I felt quietly, 'Boy, that's a tough position to put a kid in. I wish we hadn't done that.' I can't tell my coach how to coach the team. It concerned me a lot. If it's in [Alex's] best interest, it's in our best interest."

Confused and dejected, Alex faced a dark labyrinth of uncertainty. His dream seemed shattered. Could he salvage his aspirations by transferring to another school? Would another university be a better place for him? Alex consulted his parents and began weighing options.

Pam shared her wisdom with Alex. "We told him, 'Don't give up on yourself. Control those things that you can. Don't worry about the things you can't.'"

She and Doug began to believe that Alex should leave Utah and transfer to another school where he'd get a good opportunity to play. "We needed more integrity in a program," Pam said. "If that coaching staff stayed, he was leaving."

By the end of the season, Alex had come to the same conclusion on his own. The change would come at a cost, though. Following the rules of Division 1-A football, if an athlete transfers to another school he has to sit out for a year. Still, Alex thought he had no choice but to go.

Busch tried desperately to do damage control with Alex and his parents. "I had several long talks with Doug and Pam. They were upset, and rightfully so," he said. "It was a bad situation. It was a rough year for us. We should've won two or three more games. It was one of those years. Anyone on that staff would say now they would take that back if they could."

Busch told Alex's parents that heading to another school might work against Alex later. "A lot of times transferring is not the best answer," Busch said. "Most of the time, the success rate of transferring isn't very good. Plus, you want to teach your kids to fix problems and not to just go find another option."

As discouraged as Alex was, he still never lost that wide grin he was famous for in high school. "I never saw him not smile when I talked to him," Busch said.

On November 25, 2002, Hill relieved McBride of his post as head football coach. It opened a floodgate full of criticism from scores of devoted fans. "A lot of people were upset with me," Hill said. "People were loyal to Coach McBride. I have a thick file of letters from people who weren't happy."

Hill did what he thought he had to do, based on the team's performance the previous season. Hill said he didn't fire McBride because of what happened to Alex. Still, he hoped Alex and his parents would be supportive of his decision and place new faith in the program.

"We made a change. I think Alex saw it as, 'Let's give this a chance,'" Hill recalled. "It wound up being the best decision for Alex and a lot of other players. It kind of woke us up. People didn't realize we were a team that could win an outright championship."

## URBAN LEGEND

In December of 2002, Hill hired a new head coach known for his explosive energy and unique name. It was Urban Meyer. Meyer had been an assistant coach at Colorado State from 1990 through 1995. Then he served as an assistant coach at Notre Dame for several years before accepting the head coaching job at Bowling Green University in 2001.

The Bowling Green Falcons had suffered through a 2-9 season in 2000, but Meyer quickly turned the team's fortunes around. His fast-paced, highly disciplined coaching style produced results, and Meyer led the Falcons to an 8-3 season in 2001 and a 9-3 season in 2002.

Hill had noticed Meyer's success and hired him to lead the Utes. Hill had high hopes that Meyer would provide the same spark for the Utes as he had with the Falcons.

Busch advised Alex, "It would be a wise move for you to stay with a new staff coming in. You're starting at ground zero again."

As often happens with a head coaching change, many of the Utah coaches under McBride also lost their jobs, including Busch. "Initially, I was let go and I went Christmas shopping," he said.

Resigned to his fate, Busch drove to the mall in a sullen mood. While in route his cell phone rang like an early Christmas present. "I got a call and they said, 'Hey, if you want it you have a job here.' So I turned around on the freeway and went back to Utah." Kyle Whittingham was the only other Utah assistant coach that Meyer kept on his staff.

The fact that Busch remained at Utah ended up being another big break for Alex. Once Meyer took the reins, he learned that his third-string quarterback might be leaving the program. Meyer, at first, wasn't going to stop him. "Alex got misled and lost his redshirt year. His recruiting coach told me he might transfer. I asked, 'Do we want to keep him?'"

Once again, Busch spoke up on Alex's behalf. "Bill Busch was convinced he'd be a good player," Meyer said. "I knew he was a great kid with a great family but there was no indication that he'd be a great player. There was no other reason to believe that other than his recruiting coach's confidence in him."

Meyer picked up the phone and called Alex, who was back in Utah beginning a new semester but still strongly considering leaving for another university. "The first guy to call me was Urban Meyer. He apologized about things on the phone," Alex said.

Meyer explained, "I told him things would be different and there's a lot of honesty in our program."

Alex recalled, "Then he put Coach Mullen on the phone. They were worried I was thinking about transferring. If Coach McBride was going to stay, I was definitely considering transferring, but I liked Utah and the friends I'd made up there. I wanted to see what would happen with Urban Meyer."

Meyer had seemingly swayed Alex to give the program another chance, but Meyer still had to contend with two of his toughest critics.

## THE MEETING IN SAN DIEGO

The talented teams Meyer had faced as a head coach were nothing compared to the protective mother he would soon encounter in San Diego. "Pam was the toughest to convince," Meyer said. "I wanted to earn her trust."

With Busch's encouragement, in January 2003 Meyer traveled to San Diego to meet in person with Pam and Doug. "I said, 'Give us a chance. If you're unhappy after spring practice, you can transfer,'" Meyer recalled.

Pam explained, "I watched Alex's dreams shatter and people lie to him. I got kind of cynical. Doug and I were in tough positions. We were about as discouraged as you can get. Alex never got to redeem himself." What was worse, Pam suspected Alex was starting to lose confidence in himself.

Meyer did his best to convince Pam that Alex should stay. "She was ready to get him out of there," Meyer said. "I told her, 'To react now would be a mistake. There's nothing good that can come out of transferring in January. See how it goes through spring.'"

Pam listened intently. "[Meyer] said, 'I didn't have anything to do with what happened to Alex, but I apologize. Things will be different. Give me a chance. I hope he'll stay.'"

Doug said he was impressed that the new head coach took the time to travel to San Diego and talk openly with them about the situation. "He didn't defend the decision," he said.

During the rest of the conversation, Pam and Doug talked with Meyer about his plans for the offense and his goals for the team. Meyer reassured the Smiths that Alex would be given the opportunity to compete. He promised them that staying at Utah a second year would be worth it. In hindsight, that statement proved to be overwhelmingly true.

After the meeting with Meyer, Pam and Doug encouraged Alex to give Utah another try. Their support solidified Alex's decision to stay.

What had happened that year to Alex, while unfortunate, put

Alex in a crucible that could only make him stronger. His parents knew that. Even while fighting for what was best for their son, Pam and Doug never stopped looking at the mishaps as character-building experiences.

Doug said, "You have to step in and say, 'That's the way things go at times.' There are situations that go your way and there are negative things. This was one. You have to grow from it, deal with it and move on."

## SPRING BALL

Still, Alex's commitment to Utah remained somewhat tentative. "Through spring ball of that year, we were still keeping his options open," Pam said. "He could've left at the end of his freshman year had he felt things weren't going to be any better."

Meyer still kept Alex as a third string quarterback behind Elliot and Rice. He and his right-hand man, Dan Mullen, were still unimpressed with Alex. "We had come from a place where we had a very athletic quarterback," Mullen said. "We didn't think we had one."

Mullen would later become Alex's favorite coach at Utah. The two would create a close friendship. At first, Mullen doubted that Alex would be the quarterback they needed. "Alex was a skinny, gawky kid," he remembered. "I said, 'There's no way' looking at him. At spring practice, I thought he'd trip over his feet every time. But he did a good job."

Mullen thought he would give this unlikely champion some pointers. He trained Alex to change his throwing motion to quicken his velocity. "We had to lower his arm and change his delivery," Mullen explained. "We changed how he threw the ball."

His teammates noticed Alex's great potential. "We caught a glimpse of what he was going to be able to do," said Morgan Scalley, a free safety on Utah's defense. "He threw the ball differently than the other quarterbacks—it had a zip to it."

Alex was putting on the polish athletically but he still had his Achilles heel to deal with. As hard as he tried, and as voraciously as he ate, Alex simply could not keep the pounds on. Being a lightweight made him an easy target for defensive linemen. He had to bulk up in order to compete. Mullen put Alex on a strict nutritional regimen to help him gain weight.

Mullen began to admire Alex's strong work ethic. "Coming out of spring I thought, 'This kid is a competitor.' But I didn't know when he was going to be ready."

They worked hard with a new intensity level that appealed to Alex. By the end of spring semester, Alex felt good about staying. He liked the direction Meyer was taking the team. The high marks Meyer demanded of his team convinced Alex that Utah was still the right place.

His characteristic good attitude helped him through. "Alex is always the same," Busch said. "He's about the happiest kid I've ever been around. He's always smiling. That's the way he was the first day I met him. His attitude never changed."

Many of his teammates were pleasantly surprised when Alex decided to stay. "Most athletes struggle at least once during their college career," Tommy Hackenbruck said. "Almost anyone put in that situation would have been bitter and had a lot of resentment about it."

It wasn't an instant fit. While Alex appreciated his new head coach's discipline and foresight, there were different problems to work through. Urban's potency took a little getting used to. "Urban was such an intense person," Alex admitted. "It was the opposite of what we'd done the first year. I didn't like being in the same room with him because he was such an intense person."

Inside, Alex hated being rejected by Meyer. Deep down, he still believed he could be the leader they were looking for, the catalyst for a winning season. But Urban had his doubts and made them known. Alex was frustrated, but he worked on the things that he could control and let go what he couldn't, just like his parents had advised him to do. Would Urban ever gain confidence in him? Were too many things beyond his control?

"I felt like I wasn't what they were looking for as a quarterback,"

Alex said. "It was difficult for me the first six months. I didn't like Coach Meyer the first six months. He demanded so much of us. It seemed like none of us fit his ideal for the quarterback position, especially me. He wanted a guy who could run and throw and weighed 240 pounds. That wasn't me at the time. It was hard to take."

But Alex put his feelings to work on the field, in the coaches' office, and in the weight room. He used his doubts about himself as fuel to do better. By doing so, he couldn't have made his parents more proud. No matter what the future held, they were proud of his efforts to recover from the depths of despair and self-doubt.

"That lesson transcends to everyday life for all of us," Pam said. "He was working hard toward a dream. Things outside his control were turning that dream bad. He kept trying. He kept his head up. When it looked the darkest, he didn't let it ruin his life. He took control of the situation."

Alex built up his strength by pumping iron in the weight room. He spent countless lonely hours in the coaches' office watching film. Being the first one there in the morning and the last one to leave at night became his trademark.

"Right from day one he was in my office more than anyone else," Mullen said. "He was always trying to learn. I thought that would be an advantage. The other guys had been on the field longer. They had played more, but Alex really worked hard over the summer."

Back at Helix High, his sister MacKenzie was adjusting to life outside of her big brother's shadow. She learned of Alex's magnanimous efforts at Utah and applauded his courage to stay and work hard despite what had happened during the previous season.

"It would've been really easy for him to quit from there, to walk away from Utah and to walk away from football," MacKenzie said. "He took it in stride and I think it motivated him more. Being embarrassed in front of his hometown—that was the match that lit his fire to get him going. He knew what he needed to do."

Luck isn't just good fortune. It's the moment when a person who has worked hard and trained well encounters a once-in-a-lifetime chance. Alex was about to turn a corner that would change his life forever, if only he could believe in himself a little longer.

# Chapter 6

# THE SUCCESS OF
# THE 2003 SEASON

All through spring ball Alex hadn't met his coaches' expectations, and it gnawed at him like a canker sore. Summer camp began that August. There was no foreseeable way he'd rise to the helm and truly test his wings. Meyer's intensity was intimidating, and Alex's disastrous first year still haunted him. Everybody seemed to have doubts about his abilities.

"They were trying to change everything about me. I wasn't the guy they wanted," Alex said. "It was hard."

He needed a coach who believed in him like a soldier needs a captain in the trenches. Luckily, Alex soon clicked with his dedicated and likable quarterbacks coach Dan Mullen, who became the buffer for Meyer's acuteness.

"Coach Mullen and I bonded much more quickly than I did with Coach Meyer," Alex explained. "It didn't take me long to like him. I liked how he coached. He was honest. He put in as much work as he demanded. It made it easier for me to work for him."

Alex also flourished under the watchful eye of recruiting coach Bill Busch, who had priceless confidence in him. During those scorching hot summer practices, their friendship grew. "I think it's good anytime you have someone around that you're comfortable with," Busch said. "Alex was in my office area every day. We'd talk about who he was dating, random stuff. With football I just always told him, 'Stay the course, stay with it.'"

With Mullen and Busch behind him, Alex firmed up his resolve. He regained his self-assurance and the extra hours he had spent watching film were beginning to pay off.

"I got back to playing football instead of thinking about other things," Alex said. "I felt good."

His coaches were becoming more impressed. There were two good quarterbacks ahead of him, but Alex had an amazing arm, exemplary dedication, and keen intelligence. Maybe, just maybe, he'd be their starting quarterback in the fall.

Word was spreading to the top about the strides Alex was making. "The coaches would quietly tell me that Alex had the most potential, long term, to be a great quarterback," Hill said.

Mullen was starting to see the same thing in his young quarterback. "Getting into fall camp, I had a feeling that he might be our best guy," Mullen said.

Toward the end of the sweltering August camp, it appeared Alex's luck was changing. Or was it?

## ALEX'S INJURY

During his final off-season testing day, Alex's enthusiasm worked against him. Determined to prove how much he'd increased his strength from lifting weights over the summer, Alex pushed himself to his limit. He suffered a bruised vertebra and herniated disk. Ever stoic, he remained hopeful that the injury wasn't too severe. Alex planned to grit his teeth and tough it out through the pain and not let anyone know what he was going through.

Doug recalled, "He tried to hide it. He tried not to say anything about it."

But the pain increased every time he threw the football. Soon, he could hardly perform at all. For Alex, the injury was like seeing a beautiful, clear lake in the desert, then walking closer to it and discovering it was only a mirage. His dreams might vanish.

"My chance was finally there and it slipped away," Alex said. "My back was really hurting and I was thinking about redshirting."

The coaches still hadn't made a decision about who would be their starting quarterback. Would it be Brett Elliot again, his back-up Lance Rice, or the upstart Alex Smith?

While his back tormented him, the fire inside him was just starting to burn. Still daunted by Meyer, Alex waxed uninhibited in a poignant exchange on the football field. Meyer said he would never forget that conversation. "We were walking off the practice field together and he was really frustrated," Meyer recounted. "He said to me, 'If my back wasn't hurting, this thing wouldn't even be even f------- close.' He caught me by surprise. He doesn't cuss. Academics and family were important to him. But at that moment it was like nothing else in his life mattered to him. He wanted that job."

No matter how resolute Alex was about being a starter, in the end, the coaches decided that the injury ruined his chances that fall. Mullen said, "Without a whole lot of experience, it wasn't like he could sit and rest for a week and still be ready to play. That slowed him down."

## BACKUP QUARTERBACK

The season opener was against intrastate rival Utah State. The pundits and the fans wanted to see what Urban Meyer could do for Utah. No one had even heard of Alex Smith. He was way in the background as the season got underway.

Alex's back was throbbing with pain during warm up but he pushed through it. In the back of his mind, he was still considering seeking a medical redshirt so he wouldn't lose another year of eligibility while his back healed.

Still, he wanted to step on that field and show his coaches—and the world—what he was capable of doing. But after all the sweat and toil, heartbreak and hard work, would it be another disaster like the year before in San Diego?

Aware of the pain Alex was suffering, his parents watched the first game with guarded hopefulness. "When they opened against Utah State, we didn't anticipate that he'd dress for the game,"

Doug said. "We didn't think he was cleared to play, but he did dress and he even got to play."

The coaches wanted to see what Alex could do.

"We wanted to put him in the game. The first play he was in, he fumbled the snap," Mullen said. "He was struggling a little bit but we wanted to get him in there."

Alex sat back down on the bench. His season debut didn't go like he'd expected, but there was still plenty of time. The game had just begun. He tried not to let the demons from the year before discourage him.

Alex waited patiently on the sidelines. The Utes were performing well. Urban Meyer and the team were off to a thundering start. Starting quarterback Brett Elliot threw a touchdown pass at the beginning of the second half. Toward the end of the third quarter, Meyer decided to give Alex another shot. Alex warmed up his arm and prepared to go in.

This time, it could not have gone better. The crowd jumped to their feet to cheer this little-known quarterback. Alex came through, throwing two touchdown passes as Utah walked away victorious with a hearty 40-20 win.

His dad wasn't surprised at all by how well his son had performed. "He played most of the fourth quarter," Doug said. "That was really his first reasonable opportunity to play and he threw two touchdown passes. It was an ideal opportunity for him to play, even though he was going in as a backup."

The Utah coaches were impressed. Their tough sophomore quarterback had excelled at two-a-day practices in August and had played well despite his injured back.

Still, they agreed it wasn't his time to lead. Mullen remembered thinking, "We knew he could be the guy to get the job done for us. I thought that hopefully by the end of the year he could become the starting quarterback."

Still, no one predicted the turn of events this Utah team would face the very next week. Those events would change Alex's life forever.

## THE CHANCE

Utah next faced a formidable opponent, the Texas A&M Aggies, a team they hadn't played since 1936. Texas A&M was a big-time team with a new head coach, Dennis Franchione. At game time in College Station, Texas, Alex sat on the bench with Elliot as starting quarterback and Lance Rice as backup. If he didn't play any more that season, he could obtain a medical redshirt and gain another year of eligibility while he gave his back a rest. That's what he expected he'd do. But life is full of surprises.

The Aggies had a 28-13 lead against the Utes with just over thirteen minutes left in the game. The Utes later closed the gap to 28-20 to keep the game close.

Then as the clock wound down, Elliot threw 45 yards to John Madsen for a TD with only eight seconds left on the clock. Texas A&M still led 28-26, but the Utes could tie the score by converting a two-point conversion. Elliot took the snap and ran to the right, aiming for the corner of the endzone. But an Aggie defender hit him hard, knocking him out of bounds just short of the goal line. The Aggies had held on to win.

It was a fateful play for Elliot. Not only did they miss the chance to tie the game, but Elliot broke his wrist trying. Since it occurred during the last play of the game, the injury went relatively unnoticed. Alex felt empathy for Elliot, but knew this might mean he'd be able be a starter. Mullen said, "Alex was in early the next morning."

Alex and Elliot had forged close ties during practice and became confidants off the field as well. The news about Elliot's injury left Alex feeling conflicted emotionally. "I competed with Brett for such a long time," Alex said. "We became really good friends. I was sad for him to see him get hurt. It's such a hard way to lose your job. Then again, it was my opportunity and I wasn't going to let it pass me by again."

Knowing their son wasn't going to play, Pam and Doug didn't travel from San Diego to College Station to attend the game. They had no idea that Brett Elliot was hurt. They knew Alex was in a lot of pain from his bulging disc and that sitting out for the rest of the year was likely. The morning after the game, their phone rang at home in San Diego. The news they would hear next was both thrilling and terrifying at the same time.

"Brett broke his wrist. I'm starting Thursday," Alex told Pam. With her heart racing, she handed the phone to Doug.

Doug remembered, "I only knew that Utah narrowly lost the game and Alex didn't play a down."

Alex said to his dad, "Did you know Brett Elliot broke his wrist?"

Doug asked, "What do you mean he broke his wrist?"

Alex responded, "Yeah, he's out for a few weeks."

In just five days, their youngest son would be the Utes' starting quarterback. Pam was more than a little worried. "He'd only been in a few times and he had to be the starter. He came from a devastating year to a coach who was forced to go with him because of the broken wrist," she said.

## PROVING HIS WORTH

Alex's first start for the Utes would be on ESPN for the whole nation to see. He would face a mighty opponent: the California Golden Bears of the Pac-10 Conference.

With only four days of practice left before the game, Alex and his coaches got to work. Alex's injury still loomed over them. He lacked experience. He had only played for one quarter in the first two games. The coaches didn't expect greatness. They just wanted him to do well and pull off a win. "We tried to make an easy game plan for him," Mullen said.

Doug did his best to encourage him. He knew that his son's ability to focus with intensity—a plus in many respects—might also work against him now. Walking that fine line would become a skill Alex would perfect later and become known for. But before the California game, no one knew he could do it.

Doug advised Alex, "There's a fine line between trying to be too good and trying to make a play that can't be made." He counseled

Alex to not overdo his performance in this game like he'd done lifting weights at the last preseason practice. "I tried to convey to him that he was ready, that he was prepared," Doug explained. "He was well coached and I told him to just stay within himself and do what he was capable of. Don't try to do everything."

While Doug conveyed assuredness to his son, inside he was trembling a little. "They were definitely the underdog because here's a sophomore quarterback who's played one quarter of football and he's going to start against a Pac-10 team."

Before the game started, Pam tried to gauge Alex's mood. She asked, "Alex, are you kind of nervous because it's on ESPN?"

Alex answered, "No, it's good because John will get to watch it." He had a way of looking for the rainbow in the storm, and he was about to far exceed everyone's expectations.

On that Thursday night a crowd of 46,768 fans dressed in red flocked to the stadium. It was the largest crowd ever to attend a football game at Rice-Eccles Stadium.

Alex appeared to be as calm as ever, like he was simply getting ready to play for Helix High. But inside, he was nervous.

"There wasn't one game where I didn't get butterflies," Alex said. "Once I start playing, get hit a couple times, and start sweating, I lose myself. I don't hear the crowd. I just see the other players and just play."

Busch looked on with full confidence in his recruit. He believed Alex would be their stealth bomber. "The entire team and coaching staff didn't flinch at all. They had full confidence in Alex. We could win. It wasn't a problem," he said. "We knew we had a great one there who hadn't played much."

Hill sat next to his wife in their box seats at Rice-Eccles Stadium. As athletic director, he had such high hopes for his team with a new head coach and a new quarterback. "We marched down the field with Alex in charge at the start of the game," Hill said. "It was mistake-free and just what you'd want a smart team to do. Alex was at the helm. We took off from there."

Alex's older brother watched the game on TV from home

with Abbey and MacKenzie with anticipation that was hardly containable. "I thought from the beginning there's not much in Alex's game that's missing," Josh marveled. "I'd always known that if given the chance, Alex was going to erupt."

## THE OPTION PLAY

Erupt he did.

"He bit the bullet on a lot of pain and did what he had to do. He set a tone for efficiency and accuracy," Pam said.

Alex played efficiently and ran the ball into the end zone for a touchdown. The Utes led 21-7 at halftime.

"I was playing, and playing very well," Alex said. "I was happy to be back on the field. Coach Meyer and his staff brought so much energy that I really enjoyed playing football again."

Alex found his groove. All he had done to prepare mentally, physically and emotionally was coming together. "That's when the offense first really made sense to me," Alex said. "Everything fit together. I had all the pieces of the puzzle. I couldn't get the pieces together, and then finally it all clicked. The big picture of the offense, I felt like I understood so much. I felt so much more confident out there. I knew where I should be going with the ball."

In the second half, the game became iffy. The Utah defense allowed 17 straight points in the third quarter. The scoreboard showed California ahead 24-21.

Mullen said, "In the fourth quarter we were losing. We needed him to make some plays to win the game. He stepped up for two consecutive third downs as they were blitzing him, made the throw, got smacked, popped right up and kept our drive alive for a score. That tied the game."

After Alex's big play, the Utes knew they had a chance at victory. Cal punted to the Utah 37 yard line. Alex shut out the thousands of cheering fans and all the TV cameras and keyed into the game. He knew what he had to do. This was his moment.

Mullen held his breath and watched. "He led us right down the field again. With a minute and half left, he ran the option play, kept running and running and flipped it to Brandon Warfield."

Doug explained that Alex held onto the ball to make the defense attack him. Then, just before they could tackle him he tossed it to his receiver. Warfield ran with the ball for 14 yards into the end zone for the TD. The crowd roared with approval. Alex led Utah to a glorious 31-24 victory.

Busch cheered with I-told-you-so satisfaction. "That option play is one of the plays that you remember forever," he said. "Alex pitched the ball to Warfield and he ran it into the end zone. Alex set that all up. I had a feeling good things were to follow. We felt that the entire time. We knew this kid was going to be great."

Josh smiled a knowing grin. "Nothing that happened in the Cal game surprised me," he said. "There's no one playing football who's smarter than Alex."

Everything had gone amazingly well. The coaches had taken a chance on Alex and he came through. Hill said, "To win it like we did with a great drive at the end, we left that game thinking we did just what we were supposed to do."

Doug was pleased Alex had heeded his caution about not trying too hard. Sometimes, the most prudent thing an athlete can do is not make mistakes. "He performed within his scope of ability and didn't put his team in a bad position," Doug said. "You make a mistake and you turn the ball over, you give the game away. There are times you can't make a play and if you try too hard, you throw an interception. You try to make something out of nothing and you should've taken the sack. Yes, you didn't make the play, but you didn't make it worse. He didn't make mistakes and he performed well."

Alex completed 18 of 27 passes for 136 yards. Everyone was ecstatic. Alex's big grin got a little wider.

## A WINNING STREAK

The pendulum began to swing in Utah's favor. They were no longer a losing team. Still on a high from Alex and Warfield's eye-catching play against California, they kept that momentum as they played Colorado State at Fort Collins. Alex completed 17 of 22 passes for 158 yards, leading the Utes to a 28-21 win.

Next up was a home game against No. 19 ranked Oregon, a team that only two weeks before had upset Michigan. Alex's little sister MacKenzie watched the game on ESPN at home in San Diego with Abbey, Josh and a few of their friends. "Utah was down and Josh was just nervous as ever. He was sweating," MacKenzie remembered.

Early in the fourth quarter, Alex threw a touchdown pass to seal a 17-13 upset of the Ducks. Alex threw for a career-best 340 yards and two TDs.

MacKenzie was amazed. "To see Alex step in and make something happen was amazing. When they interviewed him after the game that was the first time we saw him interviewed on national TV. For that person to be my brother was awesome."

"That was our toughest stretch of the season," said Hackenbruck, who believes that game was a turning point for the whole team regarding Alex. "That whole stretch is when he emerged as a starter and took the job over. His teammates respected him, but after that we had total confidence in him. He was able to lead our team. He had the composure and he took some big hits. He was really struggling with his back. He had a lot going against him."

Hackenbruck added, "To have the poise, everyone was just like, 'wow.' He wasn't putting up huge numbers, but he was in charge of our offense and helped us win those games in a huge way. You give him a chance he prepares himself to take advantage of opportunity. When the chance came, he was ready to answer the call."

Morgan Scalley was completely sure of Alex's talent. "There wasn't any doubt as to what he could do. It was amazing how quickly he picked up on things."

The following week, the Utes beat San Diego State 27-6, and the win was very satisfying for Alex after the previous season's disaster against the Aztecs. The Utes were now 5-1 and unbeaten in the Mountain West Conference.

They then crushed UNLV 28-10, and suddenly the nation was paying attention.

Now ranked No. 23 in the polls, the Utes sought their sixth straight victory in their next game against New Mexico. But it was not to be.

Alex played well in the first half, tossing to Steven Savoy, who ran 11 yards for a touchdown. Then Utah lost their go-to player, Brandon Warfield, to a knee injury in the first half. Without their star running back, Utah made little progress and fell way behind. The Utes did put together a rally, but in the end, New Mexico beat Utah 47-35.

It was a tough week at practice as Meyer demanded the most of his team, but they didn't remain discouraged for long. In their next game they survived a three-overtime 45-43 showdown with Air Force, then the following week they blasted Wyoming 47-17. The win guaranteed them a piece of the Mountain West title. The only thing standing in their way was BYU—the Utes' fiercest rival.

## TAKING DOWN THE COUGARS

The Utah-BYU game is the kind of contest that sharply divides families for a time. It pits brother against brother. The animosity between the teams goes back decades. If you know nothing else as a Utah player, you know you hate BYU, and vice versa. The game is typically the last game of the season when both teams have reached their crescendo. It doesn't matter what kind of season either team is having—the passions are strong and anything could happen.

It was a frigid afternoon in Provo with blinding snow blowing sideways like stinging frozen confetti. It was just 19 degrees when the game started and windy. Playing that day was like trying to throw the ball with your eyes closed. Alex was operating on pure optimism.

Along with the fierce rivalry, BYU went into the game looking to continue their NCAA record scoring streak, having scored in every game they had played since Sept. 27, 1975. The Utes were playing for the conference championship and a spot in the

Liberty Bowl, but they also wouldn't mind if they ended BYU's scoring streak while they were at it.

Tempers flared as both sides fought their way through the blizzard-like conditions. Midway through the second quarter, Bryan Borreson kicked a 41-yard field goal for the Utes, giving them the lead. Little did they know that was all the scoring they would need.

When the final gun sounded, that field goal was the difference as the Utes won 3-0 and ended BYU's scoring streak. Utah also clinched their first outright conference title since 1957.

The unrelenting snow had hindered both offenses, but Alex still completed 11 of 19 passes for 113 yards. He rushed for 55 yards on 23 carries.

"That was a phenomenal year," Busch said. "They were a talented team. Alex really changed the way football was played there."

## FINDING LIBERTY

The season was deemed one of the best turnarounds in school history. The Utes were conference champions and headed to the Liberty Bowl.

After Christmas, Utah faced Southern Mississippi in Memphis, Tennessee. It was Morgan Scalley's night to shine. With less than five minutes left in the second quarter, Scalley recovered a fumble at the Southern Miss 17 yard line. Two plays later, Warfield ran it in for a touchdown.

Then with only three minutes and 24 seconds left in the game, Alex threw a 49-yard pass to Paris Warren, setting up a 19-yard field goal by Borreson and giving the Utes a 10-0 lead. Southern Miss tried to put together one more drive, but Scalley solidified Utah's win with a 74-yard fumble return.

Alex connected on only 8 of 19 passes, but he was still a key part of the 17-0 win. He also gained valuable experience playing at high stakes under the spotlight.

"Going to the Liberty Bowl was a big experience for me. I started to make a name for myself," Alex said. "It was special experience. I was playing in it and people knew what my name was. It was very exciting."

Hill was very pleased. He said, "To win our first outright championship in a long time and to do it with such good people was wonderful."

Alex's roommate and good friend Matt Kovacevich, the Utah punter, was impressed with his cohort. "When he became the starting quarterback, I didn't predict that kind of season happening—leading our team to the Mountain West championship," Kovacevich said. "Now that I look back on it, it's because he obviously works hard and does everything he has to do to make his commitment to his team."

Alex's parents were exhilarated, both for their son and for the Utah football team as a whole. "To win the league outright, and their first appearance in the Liberty Bowl for a long time—I was extremely excited," Doug said. "We were thinking: 'How does it get any better?' We thought that was as good as it gets."

The Utes finished the season ranked No. 25 in the polls, and head coach Urban Meyer was named the Mountain West Conference Coach of the Year, and was also honored by *The Sporting News* as their national coach of the year.

After spring semester his sophomore year, Alex graduated two years early from the University of Utah with a bachelor's degree in economics. He had compiled a 3.7 grade point average. His family gathered in Salt Lake City to celebrate. At the birthday dinner at a local restaurant that night, Alex wasn't reveling in his scholastic accomplishments for long. He was trying to down even more food after finishing his meal to gain the weight he needed for next fall.

The 2003 season had been outstanding, but Alex was already preparing for even more success.

# Chapter 7

# THE 2004 SEASON BEGINS

Utah had something to prove coming out of the starting blocks in 2004. Critics raised a collective eyebrow at the Utes' No. 20 preseason ranking. Was it justified? Could Utah really be *that* good? Yes, they'd won the Liberty Bowl the year before, but many people wondered how much of that success was luck. After all, a couple of those victories in 2003 certainly could have turned into losses with the wrong bounce of the football. However, these critics would soon find out Utah was a team to be reckoned with.

As the 2004 season approached, Alex sensed the pressure to achieve. "I was very anxious," he said. "The week after the Liberty Bowl I started training again. I was pushing myself. I knew what was ahead of me. I did eight months of preparation and the season was finally here. I didn't know how I'd compare to everybody else."

The team's motto for the season that appeared on local television commercials and game posters was, "You ain't seen nothin' yet." Their lofty goal was to go undefeated. They'd done well the year before. Could they build upon that and be flawless?

There are pros and cons to coming off a winning season. Hill said, "It made for a great off-season because of all the excitement building up. One of the hardest things to do in sports is to have that expectation and achieve that expectation. Everybody is out for you. Everybody looks at their schedule and says, 'We gotta beat Utah.' It's hard."

It would be a challenging but unforgettable journey.

The 2004 season would begin with a rematch of the 2003 opener against Texas A&M. Alex's brother Josh was wringing his hands with agitation. "From the bowl game of 2003 until the first game of the season, every day I pictured how it would go. I was absolutely obsessed. I knew if I could get to that day, then I'd be able to watch Alex play on a weekly basis. That was the focal point for an entire nine months. That Texas A&M game was everything."

The Utes would be facing the strong Texas team who beat them the year before, but this year the game would be played in Salt Lake City. The game was ESPN's Thursday night game of the week and would be shown to the whole nation. University officials drummed up school spirit, calling that Thursday "Utah Day" and providing hours of festivities before the game.

As kick-off grew near, a sell-out crowd of 45,419 people packed the stadium. Alex's family members were among the crowd, feeling nervous and antsy. What gave them confidence was knowing that all during the off-season the team's focus had been on beating Texas A&M.

This game would be the beginning in more ways than one. Doug said, "It was the opening game of the college season on national TV, and there was tremendous focus on Utah. They came ready to play."

## THE TEXAS A&M GAME

Alex's nerves rattled him right from kickoff. His accuracy was off, like trying to thread a needle when your hands are shaky. He barely overthrew his first couple of passes. It was a frustrating start for everyone. But it took only two plays for Alex to block out all of the hype and expectations and do what he did best. He honed in his focus and just played football.

Mullen watched with confidence from the sidelines. He knew his quarterback would come through, and he did.

"The third play of the game he threw a 70-yard touchdown pass to Steve Savoy," Mullen remembered. "I thought, 'Hey, we're gonna be pretty good.'"

Utah led 7-0 just one minute into the season opener. From then on Alex exploded. Mullen said, "He dominated the game."

Alongside his other family members in the stands, Josh screamed with euphoria. He just knew Alex could do it. Now, the world knew too. "They took the lead and never looked back," he said.

It ended up becoming Alex's best game yet. He completed 21 of 29 passes for 359 passing yards, a new career high.

The long, lonely hours of coming in early and staying late at practice were bearing fruit. Pam recalled, "He worked thousands of hours, on his own, throwing. It showed in that game. You really saw in that game that Alex was something special."

His teammates believed that Alex could do what had to be done. Hackenbruck said, "I've never had so much confidence and assurance on anything. Before every game, I was sure our offense was going to do well. We knew if we screwed up and let a big play happen, we knew the offense would answer every time."

In that important first game, Alex also demonstrated how deceptively fast he was, running the ball 13 times for 76 yards.

Scalley explained, "He's brilliant with his reads. He knows when to run the ball and he's not afraid to run it. He sees an opening and knows he can get a first down. Once he sees he can get it he can go for it. There's no fear about the kid. He wasn't nervous about getting injured."

Alex threw three touchdown passes and ran for two more TDs. The crowd was ecstatic. Their team was off to a whopping start. The Utes had shut down the Aggies 41-21.

"It was exciting to go out there and play the way I did," Alex said. "It showed me that all our work was solidified. We were doing the right thing. We could've played with anyone. We'd been questioned up to that game. We'd only played ourselves for the last eight months. We put so much more on my plate. For me, it was exciting to play that way that first week."

Hill and his colleagues and coaches had renewed enthusiasm. "It was a great way to get started," he said. "We had a packed house on national TV and we beat a top recognized team. It was a spectacular way to start the season."

The diverse and talented Utah football team rallied behind Alex. "After that first game, no one doubted what Alex could do," Scalley said. "During the off-season you saw Alex mature with his reads, with his eyes looking off defenders. To see him do it in a game was a sign he was applying what he'd learned. Once we got past that first game, we were able to relieve some of the tension. Alex felt the same way. The pressure was there to perform well, and he did."

Back in Michigan, Alex's uncle John had his own battles ahead of him as head coach. In between the busy start of Michigan State's season, John watched his nephew from afar unabashedly and full of pride.

John explained, "I stood up and said, 'Wow, this kid is pretty good. And they're good as a football team.' Texas A&M isn't a slouch. He had a big game running and throwing. Other members of our staff were giving me pats on the back saying, 'What a great job he did. That kid is something.' I said, 'Yeah, he is.'"

Alex's older sister Abbey breathed a sigh of relief after the game. "The win got the ball rolling again," she said. "It was a relief that he and the team had such a good game."

Doug foresaw an inkling of what was about to happen next. After the game, he said, "You know what? They could be something special this year. They look like a team that can play with just about anybody." With the quiet fortitude of a confident father, Doug thought secretly, "This team's for real. If they focus like they did tonight they could play with anybody."

## THE SHOWDOWN IN ARIZONA

With the impressive victory against Texas A&M, Utah climbed to No. 17 in the polls. The next week, they headed to play Arizona.

The heat in Tucson was no problem for the Utes. Though Alex had only 170 passing yards that game it was enough. He threw two touchdown passes to Steve Savoy. Plus, the defense played at their peak, doggedly keeping Arizona out of the end zone.

When the opportunities opened up, the Utah defense answered admirably, such as when a pass intended for Arizona's Ricky Williams ricocheted to Utah's outstanding defender Sione Pouha. That interception was one of many key defensive moments that helped secure Utah's 23-6 victory.

The win made Urban Meyer's coaching report card glow. In his first two seasons at Utah, the Utes had beaten three Pac-10 teams, including California and Oregon the year before.

Heads across the nation began to turn at the mention of that previously overlooked football team out West with the talented quarterback.

## FAMILY TIES

The game that followed would've been considered easy by anyone's standards—anyone except Alex. The Utes were about to play Utah State in Logan. It was supposed to be a cinch. They'd beaten them the last six times they played them. With the talent, skill and coaching discipline they had, it would likely be an easy game once again.

*Alex and his family at his college graduation on his twentieth birthday, May 7, 2004.*

Looking back, Alex was more nervous for this game than he had been for the Texas A&M game, the Liberty Bowl, or even for the mammoth Fiesta Bowl that was to come. The Utah State game gave Alex jitters like he'd never had before because it was highly personal. More extended family members and friends were attending this game than any other previous contest.

"It's the only one he let the pressure get to him," Mullen explained. "We're supposed to kill these guys but he's got 80 family members there. Playing on national TV never got to him, but he started to feel the pressure there."

You see, Alex didn't want to let down the people he loved.

The large group of family members and friends gathered in the parking lot on a windy afternoon to tailgate before the game. Runners in the Logan Marathon ran by on the streets surrounding the stadium with bystanders cheering them on. Around mouthfuls of nachos and oatmeal chocolate chip cookies, Alex's family members and friends surmised what a relatively easy game it would be for him. Little did they know Alex was shaking in his athletic shoes.

"I was pretty worked up because so many people were there to watch it," he said. "So much of what I do is because of them and for them. They're the reason I am where I am today. They're the reason I was able to play football. They're the reason I'm the person I am. You see what happens to people in similar circumstance who don't have family like I do. It made me appreciate them more. I realized not everyone had what I had."

Utah won handily 48-6 and convinced the opposing head coach that they were worthy of all the hype. Utah State's Mick Dennehy told reporters after the game that Utah was every bit as good as their impressive ranking.

Alex was just glad to get that nerve-wracking game in front of the family out of the way.

Mullen said, "Once he played that game, it was all easy from there on out."

## TAKING FLIGHT

The Utes played Air Force in Salt Lake City the next week. The game nearly sent their hopes of going undefeated crashing to the ground.

Air Force scored two touchdowns early in the game, leaving Utah fans shaking their heads with disbelief. Meyer told reporters that he was in "panic mode."

Hackenbruck remembered, "We kind of put our team in a hole against Air Force. We let Air Force drive down and score twice. Suddenly it was 14-0, but there was no panic on the sidelines. Everyone knew the offense would answer right back and they did."

It was a mighty comeback. Utah scored five touchdowns in a row. Alex ran the ball in for a TD and tossed it for two more. Air Force put up a good fight, but Utah won handily 49-35.

If any Utah player still had doubts about Alex's abilities, he was alone. "Just seeing him around—always seeing him up in the film room studying," Hackenbruck said. "Every time I was in there watching film, he'd be in there trying to make himself better. Everyone on the team noticed that. He always prepared so well at practice. That made the team have even more confidence in him."

The Utes traveled to New Mexico the following week and brought home a 28-7 win against the Lobos. Back home in Utah the next week against highly regarded North Carolina, Utah was once again victorious 46-16.

It was becoming clear that the Utah team as a whole was a unique combination. They had talented receivers led by a confident quarterback, and a solid defense. They were a varied group ethnically and religiously, they all held fast to the goal of being undefeated. And they all wholeheartedly supported Alex, who had emerged as their leader.

"The biggest difference I could see from his sophomore year to his junior year was his confidence and leadership," Scalley said. "His first year he was taking on the role of someone who was filling shoes. His second year he went out there knowing he was the man. Everyone who was in the huddle with him said he just exuded confidence. He was great leader by example."

## PERFECTING THE FINE LINE

Alex was a star on the rise. Mullen said, "Perfection became expected. That's hard to do. When people look at you, and anytime you step on the field, they're expecting greatness and perfection. Yet he would deliver. He never made mistakes."

Flawlessness was a direct result of heeding his father's words.

Doug's advice about not overreaching rang in Alex's head. Like shifting into the right gear and climbing easily up a steep hill, Alex finally understood exactly what his dad meant.

"I took on the role much more of not forcing things," he said. "It definitely paid off. I was so determined to know everything about every play. I wanted to know answers to everything so I was continually watching film. We practiced so hard. Once we got in the game, the decisions came naturally. That same focus that was in the film room was also out on the field."

It's a skill few quarterbacks ever master. Alex developed a grasp of the offense and understood he didn't have to put his team in peril in order to make a big play. He didn't have to take big risks in order to win. There was no need to try and be a hero.

His uncle John was amazed. "He lets it work for him. It's so hard to get your quarterback to understand that. When that light goes on, it's different for different kids," he explained. "The offense is designed to be a ball-controlled offense. You don't have to throw it down the field every time to throw strikes. Rather than look at number one and say, 'Throw it there regardless,' don't take that. Go to read two or go to read three. The offense is designed for one of those guys to be open. It's up to you to decide which one to throw it to. He had a great grasp of, 'Okay, I don't have to throw it there.' He knew something else would be there. He understood it. If the first is covered, the next will be open. They can't take away all three."

John held Alex up as the gold standard for his own quarterbacks and urged them to emulate him. "It's hard to tell those guys that they can throw the ball through a two-foot window—but you don't have to. Pick the four-foot window instead. You don't want to squash a kid's competitiveness and tell him he can't throw it through the two-foot window. If it comes down to it, you want him to take the intelligent choice. It's hard for kids who are that competitive to do that."

His nephew had come a long way from his clumsy first attempt at quarterbacking in the eighth grade. John had always been the mentor, the expert and a supreme talent to which Alex might aspire. It's funny how sometimes roles reverse in life, because now it was John who admired Alex.

"Watching Alex execute that offense was poetry," John marveled. "It's an artist at work. You spend all these years doing this and look at him and say, 'Wow, isn't that beautiful.'"

# Chapter 8

# THE MOMENTUM BUILDS

The drive for mastery among the Utah football players continued at a steady, frenetic pace. "The goal was to be undefeated," Alex said. "That's how I lived week to week. It was like [the movie] *Groundhog Day* but it was Groundhog Week. All I did was school and football—and mostly football, for hours and hours. Then Saturday we'd play and win. Sunday, we'd forget about it and go and prepare and do the same routine all over again. That's how we did it. We looked at it week by week. We maintained so much focus. That's why we were so successful."

But with all that concentration on football, something had to give, didn't it?

## THE ABSENT-MINDED QUARTERBACK

Alex was sometimes known for his absentmindedness. While becoming highly efficient on the football field, he was still lacking when it came to the minutia of his life. He's the kind of guy who would gladly physically attach his car keys to his head, granted if there was a way to do such a procedure harmlessly. You see, if Alex's life depended on him keeping track of his cell phone, we wouldn't have Alex for very long. He could find an elusive receiver in a blizzard, but when it came to locating his car keys he was lost.

Alex lived with his roommates in a charming, albeit messy, historic home in the Salt Lake Avenues neighborhood. The ceilings were so low in his basement apartment that he had to duck just to walk into his cave-like room. The living arrangements worked out well, though. All the roommates grew fond of Alex and even of his forgetfulness.

As Alex's fame started to grow in the news media, pesky reporters began to dig around and stumble upon Alex's quirky forgetfulness. One Saturday, Alex graciously welcomed a reporter from *The New York Times* into the rental house. He interviewed Alex about his impressive skill at the helm of his winning team. The reporter delved into Alex's brilliant mind and the fact that he had graduated two years early and was currently pursuing a master's degree. They did a photo shoot with Alex holding a football at a picturesque spot overlooking the city. It would be a glowing feature article accompanied by five photos.

Unfortunately, the reporter had to take a look around. While he and Alex were talking, the accomplished reporter noticed a scribbled message from one of his roommates on the message board. It was a note from Kovacevich begging Alex to remember to turn off the clothes iron. The reporter asked Alex what happened and then took copious notes.

Kovacevich recounted, "I went to put the iron away and it grazed my wrist and gave me a little burn. It wasn't too bad, but I still have a little mark. He did it a couple of times. We put a note on the message board, but it didn't help. He had a lot on his mind going on with the season. There was always one thing on his mind: the football season. It was his first priority."

A few days later the whole thing made the newspaper, along with a mention of Alex's piles of dirty laundry in his room. Alex's absent-mindedness was featured in a full-spread feature in *The New York Times*.

"We would always joke, 'Life's too short to do small things like that. Life's too short to clean up after yourself,'" Kovacevich explained. "He left dishes and stuff around. There was always a big stack of dirty clothes and a lot of DVDs lying around. He had a lot of junk and stuff lying around from when we first moved in."

Alex was fast becoming the star quarterback in the public eye, but at home he was still just even-keeled Alex. "He was a pretty laid back guy if he wasn't at school doing something football oriented," Kovacevich remembered. "He was just hanging out in the house. He wasn't the type who made a lot of noise. He was good roommate. He always wanted to engage in conversion and liked to have fun."

His roommate added, "Ever since I first met him, he was down to earth and levelheaded. When I met his family, I saw why. Even from the success he got, he's not going to be changed by all that. He doesn't like the spotlight as much as some other people might."

Alex and Kovacevich became good friends. While he and his other roommates joked about Alex's forgetfulness, they applauded the exact science of his quarterbacking on the football field. "No one expected him to have the kind of season he did," Kovacevich said. "It had a lot to do with the people around him. We had great supporting teammates and he was as prepared as anyone I've ever seen play. When you watched him play, you could tell he knew what he needed to do."

## THE LONG RUN AGAINST UNLV

When the newest national rankings came out, Utah had climbed to No. 9 in the polls.

On a Saturday night in late October, the Utes played at home against UNLV. The rain was coming down in heavy buckets. Fans needed an ark to get to the stadium. The deluge was so torrential that even while wearing a rain slicker and rain boots, people still got soaked. But the downpour didn't douse Alex's performance.

He threw three TD passes. Using the shovel option play that he became known for, he decided to run the ball himself in a long and memorable 70-yard journey for a touchdown. The waterlogged Utah devotees in the stadium stood to their feet and splashed their approval. Alex even surprised himself with his slick maneuver.

"It was very bizarre. I don't know how to explain it," he said. "All the sudden I was 70 yards down the field running for a touchdown, out of breath. It hit me, 'Did I just do that?' If someone would have told me I could've done that two years before, I would not have believed him. It helped me start building confidence that I can play. It was a reality check that I can."

The option play would be his secret weapon. The key was to be shrewd and little sneaky. Alex was smart and knew exactly how to pull off a fake. "It goes back to my intellectual side," Alex described. "Once I really started to grasp the bigger picture, it made it easier to make decisions. It was tape, sitting in the coaches meetings, and practicing more."

Mullen said there are many misconceptions about the option. "Everyone thinks you have to be this great quarterback to run the option play. You really don't. Some of the best quarterbacks that run the option aren't the best athletes.

"Alex is fast and a good athlete, but he's not dynamic. But he was running the option and getting all the defensive players to run to him. At just the last second he would pitch the ball. He was such a decision-maker that he would run and even when the defense knew he was going to pitch the ball, he'd wait until the last second and then he'd pitch it."

The 70-yard rush off the option play will be forever remembered by many people, including Whittingham. "He's faster than people think," he said. "He's deceptively fast, but he can move. His awareness of the defensive rush is excellent."

Scalley reveled in Alex's brilliance as quarterback. "He has the inside shovel pass he can use and he also has the option to run it," said Scalley, who made a 90-yard kick-off return on a reverse in that game.

Scalley watched with amazement as Alex eluded his pursuers on that amazing run. "Everyone on the sideline thought he'd get tackled. He headed for the sideline and cut back in and people kept missing him. Everyone started laughing when he got to the end zone. We couldn't believe that just happened. To run for 70 yards against a good defense in the rain—you don't see very often."

Sopping wet in the drenching downpour, Utah beat UNLV 63-28.

Running for 70 yards, jerking out of the defense's way and

maneuvering nimbly all the way down the field was sublime. Alex soaked it all in. "I thought, 'How many people get to do that?' It was quite an experience."

## SWEET REDEMPTION

The next week, the Utes traveled to play Alex's nemesis in San Diego. Just two years before, Alex had a humiliating start against San Diego State in front of his hometown crowd in a losing game. It cost him a whole year of eligibility and prompted him to considering leaving the university.

But not this time.

Alex ripped onto the scene during the first four possessions and never looked back.

Mullen said, "He tore them apart and had one of his best games of the year."

Utah's offensive linemen held steady and allowed Alex to showcase his skill. He threw a 5-yard pass to Paris Warren for a touchdown. Then he passed a 10-yarder to Warren for another score. Alex later found Savoy and connected on an 18-yard TD. A 3-yard pass to Travis LaTendresse had the crowd on their feet once again to celebrate yet another touchdown.

Alex threw another TD pass right after halftime, bringing his game total to a career-high five touchdown passes. Alex's game was nearly flawless. He had no interceptions and was 22 of 33 for 298 yards. Running the ball himself, he fought for 45 yards on 15 carries.

Utah beat San Diego 51-28 in a moment that felt a lot like sweet redemption for Alex. He was named the Mountain West Player of the Week, a far cry from the game that took place there two years earlier.

"I was proud of him," Pam said. "He'd worked very hard and he didn't ever quit trying. He never stopped working on things he could not control."

Then, the murmurs of breaking into the big time began. Utah's win, combined with losses by some notable teams across the country, catapulted Utah to No. 6 in the BCS rankings. That made them eligible for an invitation to one of the four most prestigious bowl games. They could become the first team from a non-BCS conference to swim with the big fish.

But to do so, they had to remain undefeated. They still had three games left, including one against BYU.

Hill said, "I thought we had a chance to win the league and move up in the rankings. I didn't even want to entertain the thought of going to a BCS game until the end of the year. I knew we had to be undefeated and not have one game where things didn't go well. I didn't think that could happen. I didn't want to start setting myself up for a crash."

Hill added, "I felt so comfortable with Alex on the field. He was so calm. I knew he knew what he was doing. He's like a coach on the floor thinking the same thing as the coaches in the film room. I knew he could do wonderful things."

## A CLOSE BOND

The friendship grew closer between Alex and his position coach Dan Mullen, who spent more time with him than anyone on the coaching staff. The bond spilled over from the football field into everyday life to a personal kinship. "There was never anything he couldn't talk to me about," Mullen said. "He'd show up at my house at 10 o'clock in the morning every time we didn't play on a Saturday and we'd watch games. One time he was still there at 10 o'clock at night watching games."

Mullen's fiancée, former Fox television sports anchor and reporter Megan West, joined them. Mullen said, "We'd flip around and watch all the games, then he'd take a nap in the afternoon and keep watching. Megan would say, 'Shouldn't you be having fun at some party?' He'd say, 'I'm having fun here.'"

Mullen was a key to Alex's success. He was the first coach Alex became close to and trusted on the new staff that replaced McBride. Mullen mentored Alex through the pressure-cooker of seeking a perfect season. Their ties to each other run deep.

"We'll always have that relationship," Mullen said with emotion. "I consider myself lucky to have been around great young men like him. I still hope that twenty years from now we'll still be close friends—and forever."

The accolades for Alex were only beginning. The week after the San Diego State game, Pam and Doug received a letter that left their hands shaky from the magnitude of the news. The letter notified them that Alex was one of fifteen candidates for the most prestigious award in college football—the Heisman Trophy.

But Alex still had a lot of hard work yet to do.

## FREEZING COLD AND A RED-HOT WIN

On a bitterly cold Saturday evening in mid-November, the Utes faced off with Wyoming in Laramie. They had beaten Colorado State at Rice-Eccles Stadium 63-31 the week before and were 9-0 heading into the game.

The bone-chilling Wyoming wind made it feel like it was 15 degrees. A power failure blackened the field as the biting gusts howled, and the outage delayed the game. For 99 minutes, fans waited in the numbing temperatures. Alex's petite mom had planned ahead. She had bought sleeping bags designed to keep a person warm in zero degree weather and climbed inside like an Eskimo wrapped up in a polar bear's skin.

Mimi Test, Alex's former assistant principal at Helix High, was right beside her. "We had mittens, with feet warmers on our toes," Test remembered. "It was an awesome experience. We waited for an hour and half before the game started. We laughed and enjoyed it the whole time. We were cold but we were having a great time."

Alex and his teammates warmed the field up quickly and turned the action up to an incandescent glow. The Utes scored touchdowns on their first five possessions, bringing Alex's season total to 27 TDs and just two interceptions. Utah burned into memory a 45-28 win over Wyoming and their hope strengthened for breaking into the BCS.

The darkness and the cold couldn't hinder their achievement. The Utes were now 10-0, with only a game against bitter rival BYU remaining in the regular season.

Pam remembered how critics had doubted Utah's credentials from the beginning. "Everyone said Texas A&M must be a terrible team. But [the Utes] weren't just winning—they were blowing people away. This year, they came out so sharp. There were several games where the second and third team got in.

"Then, you realize how hard it is to go undefeated," she said. "Even if you're a great team, there are tough weeks. It's hard to be perfect on the road in pouring rain, in 100 degrees, in freezing cold, high winds, all these different conditions."

After the game, sports reporters flanked Alex for interviews. Pam spotted a little boy who was standing with his father and holding a sign that read, "Alex for Heisman." Touched by the child's unabashed, honest support for Alex, Pam asked the boy if she could take a picture of him holding the sign. Pam explained, "I'm Alex's mom."

The child looked back at her and his eyes showed gleeful disbelief. The father explained how he and his son were avid Utah fans and had attended every single game. Pam took the boy down onto the field to meet Alex.

Test watched the tender moment unfold. "Alex knelt down and talked to him as they took pictures together," she said. "That was a magic moment for that little kid."

# Chapter 9

# THE BYU GAME AND
# AN INVITATION TO
# THE FIESTA BOWL

This Utah-BYU game would be like no other. The schools' football matchups are truly unpredictable, no matter what their season records are. Tempers flare on both sides, kindling a ferociously competitive flame. This time, there was so much more at stake for the Utes. They were vying for a monumental chance to make history by breaking into the BCS, and BYU would love nothing more than to spoil the Utes' perfect record.

Besides, the Cougars needed a victory to reach six wins and go to a bowl game. There were also rumors that BYU head coach Gary Crowton's job was on the line if the Cougars lost. The pressure on both sides was intense.

"I was a nervous wreck all week," Hill said. "It seemed crazy. It was so big."

It's more difficult in college football if you're the little guy. The Bowl Championship Series is structured so that the six most prominent football conferences can send their teams to the most prestigious bowl games, where the most money is to be made. While teams within those conferences may remain eligible to play in BCS bowls with two or three losses, a mid-major team has to have a perfect season in order to remain eligible.

The only way a non-BCS team can make a major bowl game is

to rank at least No. 6 in the BCS rankings. Other undefeated non-BCS teams had come close in previous years, but so far the BCS bowls had never had an "outsider" participate. The computerized ranking system certainly worked in favor of the "big boys." If six BCS teams have unbeaten seasons, it would be virtually impossible for a non-BCS team to be invited to a BCS bowl.

"The system is a black mark in the NCAA," Doug said. "Nowhere do you see the deck stacked that way. You don't see it in basketball or any of the other tournaments they run. The deck is stacked against you, the whole aspect of getting in."

Doug continued, "You don't play games against the BCS schools. So your only opportunity to show what you can do is in your non-conference games, which is a small number. You have to vie for this at-large bid, which is a very narrow window to try to fit into as a team that's outside those conferences."

A loss to BYU would effectively eliminate Utah from playing in a BCS bowl.

The game would be pivotal for Alex on a personal level, too. As an official candidate for the Heisman Trophy, voters would be scrutinizing every pass, carry and pivot Alex would take on the field.

"I knew this game would make or break the Heisman for him," Josh recalled. "I knew if Alex had a huge game there was a legitimate chance that he could win the Heisman."

Meanwhile, their fan base across the nation multiplied exponentially. "We became America's team," Hill remembered. "Friends called me from all over the country. We were the underdog—*The Little Engine that Could*. People looked to us and related to us as the underdog."

Even with the lion's share of people rooting for Utah, the friction between the in-state rivals made for high drama.

"I was so up for the BYU game," Alex said. "That's when the rivalry hit me. My sophomore year, I wasn't as into it. I knew you weren't supposed to like BYU. But when you live it another year, you don't find a rivalry like that anywhere else but in college

*Alex and Josh try to relax on the night before the BYU game.*

football. My sophomore year, we only beat them 3-0. We were in a blizzard. I was confused as to what was going on. I was determined to be better."

Alex's dad was so nervous he felt like he was suiting up for the game and playing quarterback for his son. "It all mounts as you roll toward the BYU game," Doug explained. "In that rivalry, it doesn't matter what you've done prior to that game because of the nature of that rivalry. It was not only the last game of the season with an undefeated season on the line, it was the BYU game. It's hard to verbalize how big that was."

From Michigan, John called Alex before the game. "I said, 'Just go take care of business with this last one and it'll be a done deal. Just take care of BYU. You can control your own destiny.'"

## THE GAME

If you had looked down upon the stadium from a helicopter on that day, you would've seen a green playing field surrounded by sheets of crimson. Utah fans packed the stadium for their team.

"Our guys were playing for a lot more than [BYU] was—a perfect season and a trip to the Fiesta Bowl," Whittingham said. "The investment this football team made over the last twelve months, you had to be there to appreciate it. The work ethic was unbelievable. It was always there. There were no peaks and valleys. You couldn't get Alex out of here. We had to kick him out about midnight. He was always in there watching. He was in there planning with the coaches right on their level. There are very few quarterbacks who have that ability."

Since Alex had demonstrated his unique ability to lead, the coaches gave him more responsibility that night than ever before. Alex would be calling plays along with executing them.

Then, it was time to compete.

Hill remembered how nervous he was at kick-off. "I was standing next to my wife at the game and said, 'You forget you're playing your rival.' It was a bigger game than that. We were playing to be the first mid-major team to go the BCS."

The Utes opened the game with a solid drive that included a fake punt, preparing the way for Alex to run two yards for a TD. But the Cougars were also playing well and kept the game close. The scoreboard at halftime showed Utah leading only 21-14. One wrong move by the Utes and BYU could catch them.

After halftime, things got very tense. After being almost spotless all season, Alex threw two interceptions—doubling the number he'd thrown that year. When BYU's Spencer White intercepted one of Alex's throws at the 45-yard line, it appeared BYU would close the gap. Alex was devastated but tried not to dwell on the errors.

"I've gotten better at not letting that take away from the moment," Alex said. "I hate it. It eats at me. I didn't think about the interceptions for too long."

Then the Utah defense came through once again. Ute defender Eric Weddle intercepted a pass intended for BYU receiver Austin Collie on the 8-yard line. Utah had the ball in prime position. On first down, Alex tossed the ball to Savoy, who bobbed and weaved through the Cougar defense and then ran down the sideline for the touchdown. That TD boosted Utah's lead to a comfortable 38-21.

Utah fans wearing sombreros and tossing tortilla chips—to pay homage to the Fiesta Bowl—lined up on the sidelines ready to bolt onto the field as the final minutes ticked away.

Abbey said, "They were pulsating to rush the field."

Alex's focus was undaunted. He threw a final 20-yard pass to Savoy, serving up a delicious 52-21 victory.

Critics called it Alex's worst game of the season, overlooking the fact that the coaches had given him a large load of less obvious, but equally important, responsibilities.

"I did a lot of little things that people don't notice," he said. "They put a lot of play calling on my shoulders and we were so successful running the ball."

Josh said, "It was the only game of his entire life where he's thrown two interceptions in one game. He knew that doesn't matter. He doesn't play the game for himself. They won the game and a chance to play in the Fiesta Bowl and that was all that was important to him."

Alex recalled, "That game was such a unique experience. I was so happy we won. It wasn't my best game, but I was happy."

## A MAJOR RUSH

The fans agreed with Alex.

An ocean of red flooded onto the field. The bleachers were empty. The fans hoisted Alex up on their shoulders and passed him around in a sublime moment of praise and gratitude. It's an experience Alex won't soon forget. "I couldn't have even drawn that

*Alex holds up a newspaper the day after the Utes' monumental win over BYU gave them an unbeaten regular season and sent them to the Fiesta Bowl.*

one out for you beforehand," he said. "To have them rush the field like that brought so much positive energy. I couldn't even have dreamt of it as a child—you don't ever expect that to happen. How many people get to do something like that?

"It helped me realize the bigger picture," he explained. "That scene at the end of the game wasn't for that game alone. It was for the entire season and what I'd accomplished. We'd come a long way. It felt good to celebrate it."

Josh was overcome with emotion by the impromptu tribute shown to his brother. "The fans said: 'Thank you for this season and thank you for everything you've done,'" he said. "That game didn't matter to them. Alex had the worst game of his life and they still carried him off the field. That's quite a tribute to Alex and what he means to Salt Lake City."

Abbey said, "He was just in heaven. It was another rare moment where you see him show a lot of emotion."

Even with all the excitement and commotion on the field, the Utah fans were a class act. There were no major problems reported that night. "To see that reaction—to see how good people were acting, the sportsmanship—that was heartening to me," Abbey said. "I've been impressed with the Utah fans."

The moment was bittersweet for Alex's family. The incredible victory was also the beginning of a good-bye to their brother. They knew the magnificent season opened many new doors for Alex. He would soon find opportunities that might take him much farther away from home, both literally and figuratively.

Pam said, "That's why we encourage so much family to come—to keep him grounded and supported. It makes a huge difference."

After the game, Alex inherited a huge party at his house in the Avenues. Hundreds of fans flocked to the house he shared with his roommates to celebrate. But Alex had his priorities elsewhere. Before joining the festive scene, he went back to the hotel to spend time with the ones who meant the most to him: his family.

## A LOFTY INVITATION

The headlines in the local paper the following day shouted "11-0." The Utes had kept the dream alive and accomplished an undefeated season.

On December 5, 2004, at a celebration at the Utah practice facility, Alex and the rest of the Utah football team learned they had officially earned the sought-after spot to play in the Fiesta Bowl, along with the honor of being the first non-BCS team to receive such a lofty invitation.

The Utes were slated to play Big East champion Pittsburgh at Sun Devil Stadium in Tempe, Arizona on New Year's Day.

But was it an equal match-up? Were the "big guys" underestimating Utah and Alex Smith once again? Pittsburgh, a member of a BCS conference, had lost three games that season and was much farther down in the rankings than Utah.

Doug explained, "Some people said, 'Shouldn't they be playing someone else?'"

Some fans wanted to see a matchup in the Sugar Bowl in New Orleans with unbeaten Auburn, but in many ways, the Fiesta Bowl was the best fit for the Utes.

"We tried to accentuate the fact that this was a wonderful opportunity," Doug said. "We had to focus on what did happen, not on what did not. They did what nobody else had done and what they set out to do and cracked into that at-large berth to go a BCS bowl—regardless of who they were going to play."

Accentuating the positive wasn't difficult for Alex. He knew that since the game would be played in the neighboring state of Arizona, many more fans would be able to make the journey. That's exactly how Alex wanted it.

"For them to be a part of it was that much better," he said.

# Chapter 10

# NATIONAL HONORS

The awards started rolling in like marbles on a slab of concrete. Alex began the 2004 season listed at the bottom of notable rungs, such as being ranked No. 18 of the top 20 quarterbacks by one national publication. Other quarterbacks such as 2003 Heisman Trophy winner Jason White of Oklahoma and Matt Leinart of the defending national champion USC Trojans were receiving all of the preseason attention. Few realized just how high Alex's stock would rise in the next few months.

By the end of the season there were so many awards pouring in for Alex that it was hard to keep track of them. Some of the most notable honors were:

- Walter Camp Player of the Year Finalist
- Cingular Wireless/ABC Sports All-American
- SI.com All-American (first team)
- Associated Press All-American (second team)
- Pro-Football Weekly All American (first team)
- Mountain West Conference Offensive Player of the Year
- Academic All-American (first team)

Then *The Sporting News* named Alex as Player of the Year. He was the first Utah football player to receive this prestigious award.

December 2004 was a memorable month for the Utes, as the team members received more major honors than any other squad in the school's history. In 1930, three players had been named to recognized All-American teams. In the "magical year" of 2004, as Urban Meyer called it, the Utes topped that record. Besides Alex, offensive lineman Chris Kemoeatu, wide receiver Steve Savoy, and free safety Morgan Scalley were also named to All-American teams.

But the award that would stand out among all others for Alex's dad was the recognition that was soon to follow. It was the Football Academic All-American of the Year award, recognizing Alex's scholastic achievements in addition to his athletic ones.

"These athletes were intended to be student athletes, as a by-product of studying for their degrees," Doug explained. "That's how it was originally intended. Academic All-American emphasizes the importance of being a student as well as being an athlete."

Pam and Doug had always stressed the importance of being well-rounded in life and focusing on education. Along with making him a better person, Doug knew that good grades meant good insurance. "His playing days are short-lived," Doug said. "It's a brief part of his life. But his continual process to learn throughout his life is going to be much more important in the long run."

Doug recalled, "I believed after his sophomore season he had the potential to get this award. It would be the ultimate recognition for him in my mind. To be the Academic All-American of the Year is something I put at the top of all those other awards."

## A FINALIST

Pam and Doug were soon at home in San Diego packing for a trip to Orlando, Florida. They were going there to be with Alex, who was a Davey O'Brien finalist at the Home Depot Football Awards broadcast on ESPN, and to attend the Cingular Wireless/ABC Sports All-American Awards Dinner.

It had been a whirlwind season of traveling to Alex's games. It had become so frenetic at times that they simply left their packed suitcase by the door when they returned home so they could use it again to travel to a game the next week. Why even unpack?

While they loaded up their suitcases for the trip to sunny Florida, the phone rang.

"We were told to pack a coat because we were headed to New York City right after that," Pam said. They had received the news Alex had been hoping for. He was one of the five finalists for the 70th Heisman Memorial Trophy, the award every little boy who plays football dreams about. It's the sport's equivalent of the Pulitzer Prize.

In that moment of excitement, Pam remembered who had brought her son to Utah in the first place. She called Bill Busch, who was now coaching at the University of Nebraska, to let him know. Though Busch had moved on in his coaching career, a part of him had remained in Salt Lake City with Alex.

"She said they'd just gotten their invitation to the Heisman," Busch remembered. "I was a mess for about five minutes. I got a little teary-eyed. I was very excited about that. I was touched because they had just gotten the information and they thought to call me."

Busch was closer with Alex than he'd been with any other player he had ever recruited. Busch said, "He's kind of like a puppy when you come home from work. 'Hey coach!' He's happy to see you. There was never a time where working with him became a pain."

Alex's uncle John in Michigan was thrilled, but not surprised by the news. "He did the right things with the ball all year long," John said. "Like Tom Brady (of the Super Bowl champion New England Patriots) in the NFL, he's never careless with the football.

"He's always been competitive," John continued. "That's the biggest thing you have to be as a quarterback. You have to be a cool leader. He developed the leadership portion. The things you do off the field are a direct reflection of how you're going to be on the field. The things he did socially and academically correspond with his leadership abilities on the field."

Memories of the "axe-handle" little boy flooded John's mind.

*Abbey, Alex, and MacKenzie sightseeing in New York City prior to the Heisman Trophy ceremony.*

*The family gathers together as they await the presentation of the Heisman Trophy.*

He remembered watching Alex fight his way to becoming the starting quarterback in high school, and then proving his worth again on a grander scale after Elliot's injury at Utah. He says all the hard work and success can be traced back to the principles Pam and Doug taught him early on.

"He goes to the field and works," John said. "He was raised that way."

And all the hard work was paying off. Still, Alex remained humble about his achievements.

Alex said, "Once I realized it [the Heisman] was a possibility, my whole goal was just to be a part of it and go. I had no expectations of winning."

The news spread like a flame on dry kindling. Alex's siblings booked their airline tickets and made plans to go to New York City. "To be able to go was a huge honor and to have my family there was even better," Alex said.

While preparing for the trip, Josh conjured up images of the little brother he used to throw the football to in their backyard.

"We would watch the Heisman presentations growing up," Josh remembered with reverence. "I've heard announcers say it's the single greatest individual award in all of sports, not just football. It makes sense. There's such a focus on the Heisman Trophy."

Abbey said, "Even people who don't know a lot about football have heard of the Heisman. To say that he's a top-five contender was amazing."

The shy little boy who got whacked by a skier on the slopes that day in Park City was headed for greatness. His little sister MacKenzie, who spoke for him to the ski patrol that day on the mountain many years ago, realized the magnitude of her brother's accomplishments while watching TV the day after the big news. "I was watching a soccer game and his name came across a little ticker at the bottom of the screen for being a finalist for the Heisman," MacKenzie recalled, dumbfounded. "I didn't know he was big enough to be on a little ticker."

## THE HEISMAN CEREMONY

It was Alex's first trip to the Big Apple and he did it in high style. He stepped out of the busy baggage claim area and through the automatic doors of the airport to a shiny limousine full of Heisman officials who were waiting to show him the town.

"The city is overwhelming alone and then you're doing all these Heisman things," he said. "It made that experience even better— being in that city."

That same day, Alex was featured in *The New York Times* once again, capping off a surreal introduction to the city. His dad could hardly believe it. "The first time you go to the city, you're in the *New York Times* going to an awards ceremony that a lot of people pay attention to," Doug marveled.

Alex's family had arrived a few days early to spend time with Alex. While sightseeing in the cacophony of lights, glamour, tall buildings and crowds of people in the center of commerce and culture, Alex harkened back to his roots that run deep.

"My family means so much to me and having them there to participate in it with me meant so much," Alex said emotionally. "A lot of the kids' families came the day of [the Heisman presentation]. My family came a few days before and we spent time together."

Abbey recounted, "We were there 48 hours and were able to see a lot of the town, such as Rockefeller Center, and hang out with past Heisman winners. There was a high school Heisman ceremony going on at the same time. People came from all over the country for that as well. To see how much these kids looked up to Alex and the other candidates was impressive."

In an amazing twist of fate, Alex's star high school teammate and friend, Reggie Bush of USC, was also a finalist and would share the stage with him. It was a long way for the two of them to travel from the halls of Helix High School.

Doug said, "It was kind of unreal. I'm an ordinary person. I associate with plain ol' people. We got there and met people you just read about and see on TV. We find out they're pretty ordinary people, too."

*Alex and Pam join Reggie Bush and his mother Denise Griffin at the Heisman Trophy ceremony.*

The Heisman ceremony itself was a momentous night. Cameras followed Alex walking down the streets of New York on his way to the presentation. All eyes were on the little-recruited quarterback who played for Utah.

On Saturday, December 11 at 8 p.m., Alex sat up on stage at the Hilton hotel with his long, lanky legs extended out before him. He was dressed in a dapper suit and tie, sitting next to Reggie Bush and Reggie's teammate from USC, Matt Leinart. The other two finalists, Adrian Peterson and Jason White, both from the University of Oklahoma, were seated nearby.

It was an hour-long special on network television to honor the best college football players in America.

"It was kind of surreal for us," Pam said.

Pam, Doug Josh, Abbey, and MacKenzie watched from the audience below. "To have him on the stage as a finalist, it was unforgettable," Josh said. "We'd thought he wasn't going to make it to the final group."

Abbey said it was pure serendipity considering everything that went right, and everything that went wrong, to bring him to that moment in time. "I thought about how lucky he was and how the hard work paid off: the new coach, the new system, Brett Elliot's injury," she said. "All these little things fell into place to get him to where he was."

Matt Leinart won the Heisman Trophy that night. He received genuine, heartfelt applause from Alex and the other candidates.

Alex's recruiting coach watched the whole event with pride. The emerging talent and genuine humility he had recognized in Alex a few years before remained intact. "Everyone's telling him how great he is and he's still just Alex," Busch said. "That's the part that's the most amazing to me, how he's handled himself through all the media. He never makes a media blunder. He's just phenomenal. He really is."

Though Alex didn't win that night, just being present and a part of the Heisman presentation was reward enough.

And his bounty wasn't over yet.

## SPORTS ILLUSTRATED PLAYER OF THE YEAR

Just a week and a half later, Alex was named Player of the Year by *Sports Illustrated*. An in-depth feature about him ran in the magazine that same week. "I was doing the Heisman and was an All-American, and all these magazines start coming out," Alex said. "I kept expecting to wake up from it."

It was the blue ribbon in a long line of prized distinctions.

Pam asked Alex, "Could you ever have imagined this would've happened?"

She explained, "If we had said at the beginning of the year, 'Let's set some high goals.' None of that would've been in [the list]. It was just amazing."

With all the accolades, it would've been easy for Alex to become self-absorbed. But there's one surefire anecdote for that ailment—your family. This was true for Alex, too. "The personalities of his brother and sisters keep him in line," said Mullen, who was also there for the Heisman presentation along with Urban Meyer. "His parents didn't let him get away with anything or give any star treatment."

Alex's uncle John was proud of his nephew's many trophies, but he felt greater admiration for the accomplishments of the Utes as a whole. "It's a great pat on the back to go to New York for the Heisman," John said. "But he'll look back and see that the things that really mattered were what happened as a football team. The individual awards are icing on the cake. It was a neat deal for all those kids on the football team. He's got a bright future."

As bright as the Arizona sun.

# Chapter 11

# THE FIESTA BOWL

After the round of award presentations, Alex now had to sharpen the singular focus he had become known for. Shutting out the glare of the media spotlight required intense concentration. It was a skill that had become Alex's forte.

"Alex put everything aside during the football season," Pam explained. "He did school and football. He focused and focused. He told Urban they needed to practice more for the Fiesta Bowl. He had a lot of pressure on him up to that game."

While coaches upped the intensity level during practice, extenuating circumstances interfered. Meyer announced that he would be leaving Utah immediately after the Fiesta Bowl to begin his new post as head coach at the University of Florida. He would be taking Mullen with him. Offensive coordinator Mike Sanford had taken the job as head coach at UNLV.

With the news of the coaching change, Alex began to consider leaving Utah after the Fiesta Bowl to enter the NFL draft. All the changes made the players a little heady and unsure at first about what was happening.

"There was a lot of uncertainty with coaches leaving," Hackenbruck remembered. "At some practices we only had two or three coaches running the whole thing." Usually 11 or 12 coaches were present at practices.

It was a time of transition and uncertainty. Yet, they were fast approaching the biggest game of their lives. They needed an axis to keep them on track.

Alex became the nucleus of the team, taking charge and encouraging teammates to retain focus.

His teammates said it worked. Everyone pulled together in a selfless display of determination and school pride.

"Those were some of our best practices," Hackenbruck said. "The players stepped up and said, 'We're not going to worry about the distractions.' The leaders stepped up. It was like having a senior, veteran quarterback say, 'We're going to have a really good practice—it's up to us. It doesn't matter if the coaches are here or not here. We want to win the Fiesta Bowl.'"

The team worked harder than they ever had before, led by the naturally shy quarterback with the disastrous start who had become the pacesetter of the team.

"He's not the most vocal leader, but when he needs to be he is," Hackenbruck said. "The intensity and the work-hard attitude was still there [at practice]."

## A BRIEF ESCAPE

That Christmas, Alex and his family gathered at their snow-covered condo gently tucked into a picturesque ski slope amidst pine trees in Big Sky, Montana. Located only an hour north of Yellowstone National Park, the pastoral setting was idyllic for the holidays. Far away from the news reporters and football fans, it was a welcome retreat. Alex needed time to reconnect with his family.

Usually, such vacations for the Smiths were a time to actively take to the slopes on skis and snowmobiles. But Alex could do neither activity. The risk of injury was too high. The vacation would have to be low key.

To poke fun at Alex's temporary fragility, his siblings and cousins cloaked him in bubble wrap that was left over from opening gifts. They sheathed him in the air-filled, cushiony plastic as a silly way of recognizing the important work he had to do.

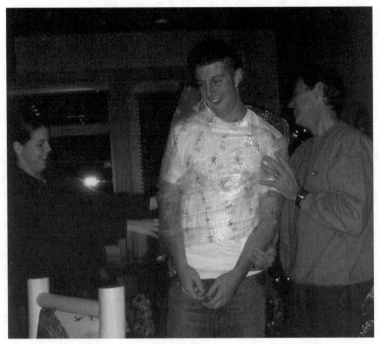

*Before the Fiesta Bowl, the family took a quick holiday vacation to ski and ride snowmobiles. But Alex was under strict orders to avoid such activities. To poke fun at Alex's temporary fragility, his family cloaked him in bubble wrap that was left over from opening gifts.*

## PRE-GAME JITTERS

The time at the condo was enjoyable but short-lived. Alex soon traveled to Arizona with the team, and the family made their way there to support him.

It was the night before the Tostitos Fiesta Bowl and the last day of 2004. Alex was watching TV with Mullen at the hotel. Mullen observed the tension that was mounting in Alex. So much was on his shoulders. He turned to him and remarked, "You seem to have a lot more pressure than trying to win this game."

Alex responded plainly, "I do."

Mullen advised, "If you go out and do what you're capable of doing, everything else will take care of itself."

Pam and Doug were staying at a hotel in Phoenix with dozens of family and friends who came to cheer for Alex. They left the party-like atmosphere of New Year's Eve to spend a few important hours with Alex. Doug had always wished Alex luck before each game and reassured him that he simply needed to "do what he'd always done and what he was capable of doing."

The eyes of the nation would be on Alex and the Utes the next night. Still, Doug gave him the same solid advice he'd given him prior to every game he'd played. "I was trying to wish him the very best, and reassure him. 'You're ready to go,'" Doug said.

## HURRY UP AND WAIT

On the night of January 1, 2005, small armies of news media in satellite trucks camped out in the parking lot of Sun Devil Stadium. As evening approached, the crowds started pouring in. The hordes were so thick people stood shoulder-to-shoulder trying to get to their seats. The confluence was a map of red with intermittent specks of Pittsburgh navy. Like the famous line in the popular movie *Field of Dreams,* "If you build it, they will come," the Utes shattered a window into the BCS and the fans arrived in droves.

"The only people who weren't at the game were BYU fans,"

Pam said. "Even a few of them were there. It was the shining star on top of it. They showed the country what kind of fans they were."

But everyone would have to wait a little longer.

The Utes were in the locker room after warming up on the field. They were receiving their final pep talks and preparing to burst onto the field when they got word that the Rose Bowl was running late and that the network would delay the start of the game. The tension mounted in the Ute locker room. They had too much time on their hands.

Mullen said, "Usually you have 20 minutes in the locker room after warm up before you take the field. We had 50 minutes."

Mullen had to think fast and use his resourcefulness to think of a way to keep Alex in pristine condition while accommodating for the unforeseen delay.

"We'll usually throw for three minutes to keep his arm warm," Mullen explained. "We had to go out during two different intervals to make sure he stayed in the flow of being warmed up. Like baseball, you gotta keep the pitcher warmed up. You can't sit for 45 minutes. Every ten or fifteen minutes we went out and kept that warmth in his body. He said he was feeling pretty good before the game and came out on fire."

Scalley remembered how aggravating the situation became. "You have a long wait before, and the media is telling you how great you are and setting you up for failure," he said. "Alex didn't let any of that bother him. He continued to prepare like he had all season long."

## THE GAME BEGINS

As game time grew closer, Hill was on the field finishing up some pre-game interviews with sports reporters. He'd been so wrapped up in his conversations with media he hadn't yet noticed his surroundings.

"Throughout the entire stadium you could see people getting to their seats with red clothing on," Hill described. "I didn't realize how big of a crowd we were going to have."

Of the 73,519 sell-out crowd of people in attendance that night, at least three-fourths of them were Utah fans.

The atmosphere in the stadium in the minutes leading up to kick-off was like a well-orchestrated rock concert. Members of the United State Air Force Academy Wings of Blue Parachute Team jumped out of airplanes onto the field. The crowd roared with approval. Between the first and second quarters, the announcer would introduce NASA astronauts Clayton Anderson, John Bennett Herrington, Scott J. Kelly, John L. Phillips, and Jeffrey Williams to accolades from the jubilant fans.

Just before kick-off, it was finally time for the Utes to emerge from the locker room. Alex ran down that small dark tunnel and onto the field knowing they'd have good fan support, but not fully realizing the magnitude. What he encountered next was a moment Alex will never forget.

"I knew our fans would travel well, since we were near Arizona," he said. "But it was amazing to walk out of that tunnel at the beginning of the game and see three-fourths of the stadium was in red. You don't realize what an effect our team had on the community and the amount of support we were getting."

Scalley recalled vividly, "The best part of that game was coming out of the tunnel and seeing a fan base that really loved our team. It was almost like we were in our home stadium. I didn't expect that much red. When we [had gone] back in, we didn't get to see how many people were going to be there. It was a sea of red. It showed a lot about our fans. We deserved our fans support and respect and they were so great."

Even with the delay and then all the hoopla, the Utah football players had full confidence in their quarterback. "He'll come up with that spark and make that perfect pass and sneak it past a defender," Hackenbruck said.

The Utes used every bit of know-how, skill and stamina they had mustered as a team. They used the shovel passes and option plays that the offense had elevated to an art form. Utah didn't let anyone down.

The Utes scored TDs on five of their first seven possessions, including three in the first quarter.

There were some blunders, too, like the play during the first half that only an older brother could love. Alex was running with the ball and had a clear shot at the end zone. Josh recalled what happened next to Alex.

"A defender got his foot and he did this spread eagle and he's parallel to the ground with his entire body," Josh said. "The ball is out in front of him and he would've had an easy touchdown. You could sense the frustration. It was more of a comical play. He barely got tripped. The guy barely got enough of him and he falls."

For Alex, his teammates and the coaches one particular play yet to come would stand out among all others.

## HOOK AND LADDER PLAY

The hook and ladder play failed miserably in practice. "We practiced it for probably three weeks just about every day," Alex said. "It never even came close to working."

Toward the end of the third quarter, Mullen decided to go for it anyway. "We're gonna call it," Mullen told Alex.

The referees called a false start penalty on the play.

Alex was relieved. "I thought we lucked out because we didn't run the play," he said. "It was such a disaster in practice."

Three plays later, Mullen called it again.

With less than a minute left in the third quarter, Alex tossed the ball to Savoy who then chucked it to Warren on the sly. Warren ran 18 yards for the touchdown. It was a truth-is-stranger-than-fiction ending to a 10-play, 94-yard drive.

Mullen said, "It was funny. I said to Alex, 'I can't believe that worked.' He just started laughing."

Alex shrugged his shoulders with astonishment. "Part of me was amazed when it worked," he said. "It put a smile on my face. When you're in a real live game, trick plays seem to have much more of an effect in the game rather than in practice."

It was a nice ending to Utah's 35-7 win.

## SWEET VICTORY

The Fiesta Bowl was a star performance by Alex, who successfully connected with receivers on 29 of 37 passes, including four TDs. His completion percentage of 78 percent set a Fiesta Bowl record. Warren set a game record with his 15 catches, and had a stellar 198 yards receiving, the third-highest total in Fiesta Bowl history.

The Ute defense was on its game too, setting another record by sacking Pitt quarterback Tyler Palko nine times.

Alex and Warren shared the offensive MVP award.

Scalley said, "Alex proved that he was one of the best quarterbacks in the nation. He proved he could do it all that game—throwing, running."

But the sweetest reward of all was the Fiesta Bowl Trophy and the knowledge that Alex and his teammates had done the unimaginable.

Mullen explained, "I saw it from the first minute of the Texas A&M game to the last minute of the Fiesta Bowl. They never let it slip. That desire to win never slipped. Their confidence level remained. That's why they were undefeated."

For Alex, the moment of victory was flawless. All the attention and praise that has followed was hard for him to comprehend.

"It is an absolute trip," Alex said. "It feels so surreal for me. I think I grew up so average—and it drove me. Even in college. Now all of the sudden to be talked about in the way I am, it's hard to put into words. I'm just so happy. I'm so thankful for my life."

Hill remembered being up on the stand with Alex during the presentation. "Our players' faces were beaming," he said. "Alex was thrilled."

Hill knew that the win increased the probability that Alex would be leaving Utah. With gratitude, he turned to Alex. "I told him that we appreciated everything he'd done and that whatever he decided to do he had our full support. He represented the best of what there is in college sports."

Pam was happy for her son. "He got to enjoy the moment."

Doug said, "They didn't waiver from that focus. You'd expect teams to have a letdown during the season. They didn't. There wasn't one game where you'd say they didn't come well-prepared to play. They were ready every week."

What made it even more special, perhaps, was that Pam and Doug in their wisdom knew that what was happening on the field at that moment was a once-in-a-lifetime experience that Alex would look back upon fondly his whole life.

Scalley said, "It's something that I'm not quite sure we'll realize how special it was until ten years down the road when we have kids. It's something you dream about as a kid. For it to be a reality—it numbs you and you don't realize how special it is until later on."

# Chapter 12

# MOVING ON TO THE NFL

It was time to say good-bye.

The world of the NFL would be Alex's next playing field.

Alex had accomplished far beyond any goals he had set for his time at the University of Utah. His achievements surpassed his wildest dreams.

He had already earned his degree in economics two years early. Favorable conversations with several NFL teams and long heart-to-heart discussions with his family led him to plant the seed that had first germinated in his mind after the BYU game. Alex was leaving.

## THE ANNOUNCEMENT

On Tuesday, January 4, 2005, Alex held a news conference inside the Spence Eccles Fieldhouse on campus. With cameras rolling and shutters flashing, Alex told a throng of reporters he was saying good-bye to Utah to move onto his next challenge in the NFL.

It wasn't an easy decision for Alex. He was leaving the people he had grown to love and an experience that was matchless.

But the timing was right and he had the full support of the coaching staff. Kyle Whittingham, who was named the new Ute head football coach replacing Meyer, sat by his side at the news conference. Whittingham told reporters that if Alex were his son he would have told him to do the same thing. As much as

Whittingham wanted him to stay, he knew the best thing for Alex was to go and allow his new career to take flight.

"He's a unique kid," Whittingham said. "To have the whole package, the work ethic—there is no weakness in Alex Smith. He's still tough as nails. All you gotta do is tell him what he needs to do and he'll do it. He's as good as you'll find character-wise, humility-wise: A+. I wish him the best. I think he's made a great decision."

Hill also focused on the tremendous positives that remain for the Utes even with Alex leaving a year early. He remarked that Alex would be an incredible alumnus and the benchmark impression he left behind would last forever. "It's what drives you to do what you do—to be around people like that who have seen their dreams come true," Hill said. "I tell people about him and people say, 'No, that's not true, he can't be that good of a guy.' But some things aren't too good to be true. This one is true."

Alex was smack in the middle of a whirlwind few days. Pam explained, "He flew up to Salt Lake the next night [after the Fiesta Bowl], did his press conference on Tuesday, drove back here on Wednesday, made a decision on an agent Thursday, and by Sunday was on a plane to Florida to start training for the NFL draft."

His older brother put a protective wing around Alex. While Josh fully supported Alex's decision, he was sorry to see him leave college football. "He's leaving this thing I love so much," he said. "It was sad. We're moving up and moving on but we're moving into something that's not as innocent. It comes with worries about people trying to take advantage of him. The NFL is such huge money. I want him to be able to return to Utah at any time as loved as he ever was."

## FINAL RANKINGS

The unlikely star quarterback at the University of Utah had risen to greatness.

The Utes finished the season as the No. 4 team in college football. Alex led Utah to a 12-0 record and the Bowl Championship Series. He was 21-1 as quarterback with 16 straight victories over two seasons. In his final season alone, he racked up 3,583 total yards of offense, completing 32 TD passes and ran for 10 more. The 2004 Utes scored 45 points per game, making them the highest scoring team in Utah history.

None of it had come easily.

"He got better and better every single way all the way to Fiesta Bowl," Mullen said.

The conversation Pam and Doug had at the Utah State game with Coach McBride's wife two and half years before had indeed proven prophetic. Many say Alex was the best player ever to play at the University of Utah.

He was smart, too. His braininess will likely set him apart from others in the NFL. Doug explained, "Even more so than years ago it has become that quarterbacks, more so than other positions, have to be cerebral. They have to be able to think about, study, and apply concepts on the field and analyze them off the field. It's a mental game, too."

He'd come a long way since the days of using Bunsen burners in AP chemistry at Helix High.

## SAYING GOOD-BYE

The lanky boy from San Diego with the big feet, warm heart and a close-knit family had hurdled over the obstacles in his way. It was because he had a soft place to fall.

"That's what held him strong through everything—the family," Busch said. "How he was raised was a huge part of his success. You have so many ups and downs [in college football]."

Alex was not a prodigy. His first performance as quarterback for Pop Warner in the eighth grade was meager. In ninth grade at Helix High, coaches remembered Doug recommending Alex run cross-country track instead. But Alex worked hard honing his skills and beginning a work ethic that would later make him famous. He earned two championship titles with his Helix team but remained in the cool shadows of his teammate Reggie Bush.

College football recruiters largely overlooked Alex.

One coach saw a luster in him through the tarnish. Sometimes it only takes one.

At the University of Utah his first year he persevered through a coaching decision that nearly knocked the wind out of his dreams.

"He went through a rough time his freshman year and had legitimate reasons to be upset. But he kept it even keel," Busch said. "Alex is always the same. He's about the happiest kid I've ever been around. He's always smiling. That's the way he was the first day I met him. His attitude never changed."

Scalley concluded, "It was tough to see him put in the San Diego State game and lose his eligibility. He's proven he didn't need that extra year. He's made the best of it."

He began his sophomore year as a third-string quarterback but he took the reins after Elliot's injury with finesse and grace. "Alex holds Lance Rice and Brett Elliot in the highest regard," Pam said. "They were competitive players and here the young guy comes in and takes the job. They did nothing but support him. He learned a lot from how supportive those guys are."

He remained humble while his successes mounted, even when he began collecting football awards like a child collects rocks in the back yard. Alex led the Utes to their best season in the university's history. He became one of the premier college athletes in the nation. All the while, he remained the nice guy with the big grin who loved everybody.

Busch commented, "You don't see many people who are as successful athletically and have his personality. Some guys are just jerks. You have to have an edge to be competitive. I've never seen a guy being that competitive and that popular at the same time. I can't imagine other teams being anything but complimentary of him."

No one could be more proud of Alex than his family.

"Alex has earned every second of this," MacKenzie said. "There's not a better guy out there for people to look up to. He's the fairytale story. He worked hard and wasn't handed anything. Alex put hours and hours into football. He truly understands the game. It's an amazing accomplishment to master the game. I couldn't be happier. There's no bitterness or resentment from his siblings. We all feel like it's happening to all of us."

The halls of Helix Charter High School will long whisper his praise. The assistant principal who watched his metamorphosis noted, "His success was opportunity, choice and effort. When he got to Utah, he was the same person," Mimi Test observed. "He still chose to make the effort. It became more of a Cinderella story. How can a kid who began as Utah's third-stringer make these things happen?"

Test and some of Alex's high school coaches were present for the big moments of his college career—the frigid game in Wyoming, the groundbreaking Fiesta Bowl debut and the hallowed ceremony in New York City for the Heisman. "It was: can you believe, can you believe, can you believe?" she said.

His mom believed, "It takes a village to raise a child."

It took a group of loving parents, devoted family members, untiring coaches, talented teammates and faithful teachers to raise a champion.

"There are a lot of things that had to go right to get me here," Alex said with gratitude. "You have to take advantage of it when you get the chance. But I've been so fortunate to have the family I have and to live the life that I've lived. Now to embark on a new phase in the NFL . . .

"I have so much to be thankful for."

# ABOUT THE AUTHOR

© 2004 Kent Miles

Heather Simonsen is the author two novels: *Sugar House Hill* and *Horseshoe Bay*, and she writes for *The Salt Lake Tribune*. She has been featured in *O, The Oprah Magazine*, and *First for Women Magazine*. Heather was a spokesperson for the 2002 Olympic Torch Relay and was responsible for selecting 100 honorary 9-11 torchbearers. Heather was a torchbearer and ran with the Olympic Flame in San Antonio, Texas, the city where she grew up. She was a full-time celebrated TV reporter for five years in Salt Lake City before leaving the profession to raise her kids.

A senior fellow honors student, Heather earned a magna cum laude bachelors in journalism from the University of Texas at Austin and a master of arts from Brigham Young University.

She has an identical twin sister, Holly, and three brothers. Her father studied at Stanford University and is a department head and professor at Texas State University. Her mom, Julia, is a homemaker and a family history researcher.

Heather has two children, Halle Rose and Christian. Her husband, Soren, is an award-winning architect and city planner. The two remodeled their historic English Tudor style home in Salt Lake City. Heather is Alex Smith's first cousin.